STOP

KILLING ME

BLACK MAN

BLACK ON BLACK

DEATH

&

DESTRUCTION

Rev. Anthony Martin

20 Time Author-Inspirational/Motivational

Speaker

The Kingdom Culture Fellowship Ministries
& Christian Self Publishing Co.

STOP KILLING ME BLACK MAN
BLACK ON BLACK DEATH AND DESTRUCTION
By REV. ANTHONY MARTIN

Printed in the United States of America

ISBN 978-1-63273-003-9

Unless otherwise indicated, Bible quotations are taken from
The Kingdom Culture Exploratory Study Bible
The Kingdom English Standard Bible.

The Kingdom Culture Fellowship Ministries
& Christian Self-Publishing Co.

www.thekingdomcultureblog.com

This Book is dedicated to:

The

Millions of Black Men that has fallen

to a senseless lost that

occurred by the hands of

A

BLACK MAN

BLACK ON BLACK

DEATH AND DESTRUCTION

A NATIONAL THREAT

TO OUR

SOCIETY AND SOVEREIGNTY

OF THIS GREAT

NATION

Part I: Why Are You Here

Part II: Stop Killing Me Black Man

A Message to the Black Man
Choose to be Black Man

THE COLORED SOLDIERS

If the muse were mine to tempt it And my feeble voice were strong,

If my tongue were trained to measures, would sing a stirring song.

I would sing a heroic Of those noble sons of Ham, Of the gallant colored soldiers

Who fought for Uncle Sam! In the early days you scorned them,

And with many a flip and flout Said "These battles are the white man's.

And the whites will fight them out."

Up the hills you fought and faltered, In the vales you strove and bled,

While your ears still heard the thunder Of the foes' advancing tread.

Then distress fell on the nation, And the flag was drooping low;

Should the dust pollute your banner?

No! the nation shouted, No! So when War, in savage triumph,

Spread abroad his funeral pall Then you called the colored soldiers,

And they answered to your call.

And like hounds unleashed and eager

For the life blood of the prey, Sprung they forth and bore them bravely in the thickest of the fray,

And where're the fight was hottest,

Where the bullets fastest fell,

There they pressed unblanched and fearless

At the very mouth of hell.

Rev. James Cunningham

REVIEW

Rev. Anthony Martin dissects the principle issues with Black on Black Death and Destruction, from a biblical perspective from the Old Testament through to the New Testament and gives extraordinary knowledge, understanding and wisdom to the plight of burden upon the black man's way of exercising survival skill, living in this world as citizens of the Kingdom of God. This stirring and compelling book will surprise readers who think they have heard all they need to know about this complex issue of Black on Black Death and Destruction, the Black family and the church family faces on a daily bases.

- *The opening content of the book (The Colored Soldier and Introduction) is a very effective launch pad for the Book. Readers will immediately become engaged in the content through learning something from a different view points with the use of historical events as in slavery, systematic racism and much of the "Civil Rights" era. Giving the reader more to think about with this indebt wisdom. The opening pages will capture and hold the readers' attention, which gives the book a lot of potential to assisting many who still in search a solution to this complex issue still needs to be addressed today.*

- *The author crafted his discussion very efficiently in that he chose just the right words to show the connection between God's Devine purpose and plan in our lives.*
  Many communities, Christians and non–Christians have a very hard time making connections between spiritual principles and their every day experiences. Readers will definitely have much more wisdom as to what we face with this complex issue of Black on Black Death and Destruction, thanks to the author's stellar message that is surely needed in this day and time.
- *The entire book is replete with references to Bible verses, which shows all readers, whether they have been walking with the Lord for many years or know nothing about Him, that this book is 100% based on God Himself, not any religion, or some movement, but a source of Spiritual Inspiration & Motivation, that someone seeking an answer can find what they need in the knowledge, understanding and the wisdom of this Book………………………………………………………*
- *The author's clearly possesses thorough Godly wisdom to Be used as God's instrument to communicate to Gods beloved Royal Family…………………………………….*

GODS PREDESTINATION

The bible gives the first and only true account of the origin of mankind. It is the only book containing an accurate record of the progress of man toward civilization, and it is the indispensable reference of all searchers after the real facts of the birth of humanity and its progress toward the civilization of today; beginning with his creation, it is the only authentic record of man; authentic because it is first hand, not a copy of something else or a scientific or literary review, but a dispassionate record of man's creation and progress, untrimmed, unshaped and unvarnished, to suit prejudice. It would not be a complete record if it did not show the origin of the black man and "Woe for all those history thieves"—it shows that he, the "black man" is the "Father of Civilization." The black man has been misrepresented by prejudiced historians and lecturers. As quoted that Ham the son of Noah also as noted the father of the black man, was cursed by his father, "For he cursed" Ham, although he did in a fit of intoxication pronounce a curse on Canaan, the son of Ham. Canaan was the Father of seven prosperous nations; foremost among them were the Canaanites, Phoenicians and Sidonians. The Sidonians sprang from Sidon, who was the first son of Canaan, according to Genesis 10:15. These Sidonians are the men "descended from black men" whom Solomon ordered Hiram of Tyre to engage to do the skilled hewing and designing of the timber work on Solomon's temple—Solomon declaring that these Sidonians, "black men" were the only men possessed with anywhere near sufficient skill to take charge of and successfully complete the artistic timber work on "His" Solomon's temple. 1 Kings 5: 6 speaks very plainly of this fact. Solomon knew the black race was a superior, not an inferior race. He married Pharaohs daughter— 1Kings 3:1; 7: 8, 9: 16. Solomon's wife might have been of as dark skin or even as black as he was, for history shows that Egypt had two full blooded Ethiopian Pharaohs just before and during the reign of Solomon, according to Herodotus, the names of these two Ethiopians were Sabaco or "Sebichos" and Sethos, so Solomon surely got an Ethiopian "Moor or black" woman for a wife. This naturally increased the proportion of Black blood in the veins of many race communities abroad.

Viewing the progress of the immediate descendants of Ham we learn that a curse laid upon one was a disgrace, according to the Bible. Although black men displayed the greatest brain work and wisdom ever given to this world at least in whose veins the greatest portion of blood was Ethiopian Moors or Black blood. As to this assertion and King Solomon, 1 King 1: 6," Solomon's skin tone should cause no surprise, because his mother, Hittite, was also the widow of Uriah (2 Samuels 12: 9-10). The Hittites are the descendants of Heth and Heth was the second son of Canaan (Genesis 10: 15). Jesus, Our Blessed Savior of Mankind, head is covered with woolly hair as he returns to judge the world, (Daniel 7: 9-10). Now, if Daniel's prophecy is true that when Christ left this earth he had woolly hair, he naturally will return with woolly hair, and the pictures of Him today are an erroneous conception of Him, by the artists. The fact remains, however, that regardless of what has been said and done against Black Men and of whatever might be said or done against him in the future, he is the ONLY man who can trace himself back through the ages to his origin, and find monumental evidence of his unequaled greatness, his prowess, the laurels and great honors he won, the things he created and perfected which have a direct influence on our civilization of today. The "black man" is the Father of civilization," born in the land of Egypt, and the different branches of Science and Art were simply transmitted to other races, which, as the ages have rolled by have only been enlarged and to some extent improved upon. Even the modern African American Man has proven that he is original, for instance—as an Artist he has no superiors and no Black Man was ever known to enter a "Barber College" to learn the trade. Black Men inherit the most musical voices, and if you have not heard a Black Man quartette or chorus after they have arranged the harmony of a piece they are to sing, you have not heard what is best in vocal music. As instrumentalists "not forgetting the many others" I simply mention Marvin Gaye, and Donny Hathaway, the fame of these two men needs no comment. They only displayed that talent handed down to them through centuries by their black ancestors. As for the Black Men being original, why the Black Man has given greatness to America, the only claim she ever did or ever will have to a National music. God honored the black man by allowing some of his Ethiopian Hebraic blood to flow in the veins of His only Son Jesus Christ, and assert that Jesus would in America be classed a NEGRO.

This assertion is only on the authority of the Bible, according to which Jesus was born out of the tribe of Judah. Judah had only five children and they were males, (1Chron. 2:4), three by his first wife and two by his second wife (1 Chron. 2: 3, 4), and both of his wives were descendants of Canaan, a black man who was the son of Ham (Genesis 10:6). Tamar, Judah's second wife, bore him two of these sons whose names were Phares and Zarah (1 Chron. 2: 4), these two names appear in the genealogy of Jesus Christ in the Book of Matthew, so it is no trouble to see that Judah of whom Christ was to come, started out by presenting to the world children of Canaanite women who were Hamite descendants. Now, Virgin Mary, of whom Christ was born was beyond all doubt a woman out of the tribe of Judah, and every Bible reference proclaims that Jesus was to spring from this tribe of Judah (Genesis 49-10, Heb. 7-14, Rev. 5:5). Paul tells us in (Romans 1-3) that Jesus was of the seed of David according to the flesh. David is the 10th man named from Judah in the genealogy of Jesus Christ (Matthew 1: 3rd, 4- 6). Added to this David's great, great grandfather "Booz" was born of the woman Rahab, who was a direct descendant of Ham (Matthew 1:5). This also shows that David, one of God's greatest soldiers, was one who most successfully led his people and one who had Negro blood in his veins. Bible history is full of honors for the Black Man, Jethro the Ethiopian or Negro father-in-law of Moses, who was the author who first employed that, which is today, our judicial system, considerably twisted and revised to meet the changing conditions of civilization (Exodus 18;). This chapter tells of Jethros visit to Moses, and how he gave Moses the foundation of what is today our system of graded courts for pronouncing judgments. Again Moses "The Hebrew Emancipator" was named by a black woman "Pharaohs daughter"—she said she called him Moses because she drew him out of the water (Exodus 2-10) and besides black men educated Moses. At any rate he received what education he had in the schools of the Moors (original for black) of Egypt (Acts 7: 22), so there is nothing remarkable in the fact that Dr. Booker T. Washington, W. E. B. Dubois, W. S. Scarborough and many other Moors or black men occupy places among the foremost and most eminent educators of the world They are descended from the Ancient Fathers who ruled Egypt centuries ago and with their great wisdom laid the foundation of learning.

PART I

WHY ARE

YOU HERE

CHAPTER I

The Reason to Live

Black Man

T ime changes all things" is a saying so old and so true as to admit of no argument. It is exemplified in so many different ways as to require no comment, and yet when we hear the phrase used thoughtlessly, every day, it is but natural to wonder if the one who uses it realizes what he is saying, or rather, if he knows what those few common place words mean, when used to form that sentence. It is a foregone conclusion that he does not. He never stopped long enough to examine even a little of the abundance of indisputable proof that the saying "Time changes all things" applies to things and conditions, seldom if ever present, to this narrow mind, and far away and beyond even this low prejudiced influence. When we hear or read the sayings of some of our "misnamed" great men, in reality, we are fully justified in making the charge of falsifying and concealing such facts as they are not really ignorant of. One of these conspicuous public characters delights in making the assertion that the Hamite Ethiopian or Negro never amounted to anything, or possessed anything, never occupied an eminence, save to which the Semitic or Anglo-Saxon had dragged or driven him up to. If ignorance alone was responsible for this glaring falsehood, a great deal of sympathy would go out to those who make the statement as well as those who believe it to be true because of ignorance.

Much of the wisdom is self praise for successfully concealing, or at least surrounding historical facts with such theory as to place the descendants of Shem upon an eminence which is justly his according to the blessings of Noah and makes him appear much larger than what he really is. Some knowledge of the origin of mankind exists, and it is this knowledge that causes the falsifying of much as possible the true historical records, especially of the black man. It cannot be said that the learned historical writers, the great Divines, Theological students and lecturers of today lack in knowledge of the history of Ham, the son of Noah, and his descendants, such as Nimrod, the founder of the great ancient city of Babylon, and also Menes the first King of Egypt and the founder of the great ancient city of Memphis. Ridpath says that the traditions of antiquity points to Memphis and Babylon as the fountains of human wisdom. If those above-named are ignorant of the history of the last-named, they are doing the world a great injustice in assuming the position of teacher and leader. If they are familiar with the history of the races and the deeds of men, they will no doubt have for them and their kind good and sufficient reasons for making false and misleading statements as to some historical records, and totally forgetting others. An early Queen of Egypt was a descendant of the Ethiopian or Moor race. This is conceded by some of the modern writers; some of them going so far as to say that her skin was very black, and a few of them acknowledge that it was this black queen who placed the first fleet of war ships on the river Nile. They have no doubt traced this woman back to where they are satisfied that she was descended in a direct lineal line from Zipporah, the black and Ethiopian wife of Moses. We read very little of these two women, because modern writers seek to obscure them, and Many of your Pastor, Preacher, Teachers never preach or lecture on that part of the Bible in which they are mentioned. Simply because if they do, they must give credit to black race. In this Biblical history it could begin even with Hannibal, the Carthagenian General, and record the accomplishments of black men without the intervening of any long periods of time, down to the time of Alexander Dumas, Toussant L'Overture, and Alexander Sergievitch Pouskin, Russo-African poet. The borders of this Republic and beginning with Crispus Octikus, or Alexander Hamilton—record the accomplishments of these same black descendants of Ham, down to this day. This modern record would contain many references to both the war of Independence and the war of the Rebellion. It would also mention a great many black men that one can never forget El Caney and San Juan Hill. Besides the heroes of war, modern history is replete with the names of black men famous in peace for their accomplishments in science and letters of art.

Not to mention Frederick Douglas who was one of the greatest statesmen America ever had, even though he was born a slave. Dr. Booker T. Washington was also born a slave, and is one of the greatest educators the world has ever known. As to the many other great things black men have done and are doing. Mr. Matt Henson, the Moor, who indeed, was one of the first of the only two "to date" to reach the North Pole. God revealed civilization to Noah and his three sons, Shem, Ham and Japheth (Gen. 9:1), and it became their duty to start to work on the first moves of the puzzle, as well as to create nations. He, who would begin from the first, moves and works the matter out to perfection. Ham, the father of the black man, located in Africa was his homestead, so to speak. David, the Psalmist, credited Ham with this territory in the 105th Psalm 23-27, and also in the 106th Psalm 22. Cush, Mizriam, Phut and Canaan were the first sons of Ham (Genesis 10: 6), and these four sons including Nimrod, the grandson of Ham, were the first to start work on the problem of civilization; in the word they were the pioneers and the very pillars of civilized governments. Cush located in South Egypt on the River Nile. He became the father of the Ethiopians as well as the father of the Cushites through Nimrod who located on the Southern part of the Euphrates River. It is to be remembered that Nimrod is the founder of the Babylonian kingdom (Gen 10:10) Mizriam located on the upper part of the River Nile, and he became the father of the Egyptians Moors. Phut located in the Northern part of Africa. Canaan located in the land known as the old Palestine country, which is modern Turkey. Canaan became the father of the Canaanites (Gen 10:15, 16-19). The question is, "Was civilization born in their land and given birth by Ham's first offspring?" It is conceded by John Clark Ridpath and a few other writers on ancient history that the Egyptians were the fathers of civilization, according to the chronology of Manetho, an Egyptian priest. Egypt was founded in the year 3892 B. C., and Menes was the first mortal King. We learn from the Bible that Ham is the father of the African family; the Ethiopian is the darkest or blackest tribe of the Hamites. Cush was the founder or father of this tribe. Moses selected his wife from this black or Ethiopian tribe (Numbers 12:1). The Bible contains the only authentic, and certainly the most ancient record of not only the Egyptians, but of all mankind.

According to the Biblical Gazette, the word "Egypt" is derived from the word Mizriam, and this word "Mizriam" was the name of one of the first sons of Ham (Gen 10: 6). By the word "Egypt" being coined from the word "Mizriam," it strengthens my contention that the Egyptian was descended from the black man. Viewing the ancient Biblical map of Africa and Asia, which Shem, Ham and Japheth first located, you will notice that Mizriam, the second son of Ham, and the accredited father of the Egyptians located where the great City of Memphis was built by Menes, the first King of Egypt. Again you will notice that all the names within African borders are names of the sons of Ham, Shem and his offspring, located in Asia. All of the Anglo-Saxon men located in Asia and according to the Bible never began to travel in Africa until Abraham's time, B. C. 1921. The Egyptians lived in a high state of civilization near 2,000 years before Abraham's first visit to Egypt, and the appearance of Anglo-Saxon people was a circus and a curiosity to the black nation. Abraham realized this fact and commanded his wife to represent herself as his sister, because as he said, "she was fair to look upon," possible Caucasian (Gen. 12:11-13). Until after the time of Abraham, the Egyptians were a pure black race. Shortly after Abraham's visit, the Shemitic travelers began to pour into Egypt to such an extent that the Egyptians began inter-marrying with them, and of course, this inter-marrying had its effect of contaminating the pure Black blood, and this inter-marrying was the cause of the black man, or full blooded Egyptian Moor to lose the power of control in the Kingdom. In other words—this is the loop through which the Shepherd or Caucasian or Shemitic kings slipped through and took possession of the Egyptian kingdom Empire.

DR. W. E. BURGHARDT DUBOIS

Dr. W. E. Burghardt DuBois is the most scholarly speaker and writer of the Afro-American race. He is the author of the book "Souls of Black Folk," which is a marvelous book. On the following page are some of the phrases from his famous address to the Social Study Clubs of Chicago University.

February 13th, 1907, on Education and Civilization:

"The doing of the world's work is a great duty and a great privilege. It is a thing not to be aimed at but to be aimed   beyond. Just so soon as a nation or a country can put its foot upon this satisfaction of the lower wants and step upward to the greater aspirations of human brotherhood and the broader ideals of civilization, just so soon the real building of civilization begins. It seems to me, therefore, that the students of Chicago University and they that teach them, ought especially, on every occasion to impress this broader aspect of the race problem. That instead of putting it in its narrower, nastier channel, instead of stooping to listen to men, who themselves represent what is lowest and least in our national organization, that you should strive in every way to realize yourselves and to show others that this great broad question of humanity is not a question of petty crime, not a question of so many bales of cotton, not a question even of mere industrial development, but is a question of human aspiration, and that if here in America, on the very fore front of present advance, it is possible to murder the aspiration of 10,000,000 of men, then America is not yet civilized."

Dr. Leonhard Schmitz, Ph. D., LL. D., F. R., S. E., says in his work on ancient Egyptian history, that these Hyksos or Shepherd Kings were Semite people. "White," and they comprised the 15th, 16th and 17th dynasties, which covered 511 years. Now, during this period, Jacob and his twelve sons and their families moved from Canaan to Egypt, and other Semite or whites from Asia did likewise, because Anglo-Saxon men had begun to rule Egypt. At the 18th Dynasty, however, fortune turned against the white rulers of Egypt, and the Moors or the Negroes regained possession of their country, and banished the whites from their land, except the Jews, whom they held as slaves. They reorganized the Kingdom with their own blood, "the blood of the Moors." Aahmas was the first King after the Anglo-Saxon were driven out, and his wife was Nefruari, the Ethiopian Princess, greatly celebrated for her dusky charms, her wealth and her accomplishments. The beginning of this reorganization of a period is recorded in the 1st Chapter of the Book of Exodus, which shows that at the beginning of the slavery of the Jews, God told Abraham that his people would be held in bondage in Egypt for 400 years (Gen. 15:13). Those 400 years marked the period of Egypt's most rapid and substantial progress, as Dr. Schmitz says in writing on ancient Egyptian history, those years were the most brilliant in Egypt's record, and the period at which her art reached its highest point. It is but reasonable to suppose this to have been so, for the Shepherd, or "Anglo-Saxon Kings" had destroyed all of the former brilliancy of Egypt, and did not because they could not do anything to replace or imitate its grandeur or beauty.

The Egyptian Moors when they regained possession of their Kingdom and again began to rule, made slaves of the Jews and compelled them to do all the heavy, dirty, unskilled labor, such as carrying bricks and mortar and working in the field (Exodus 1:13,14). While the Egyptians turned their attention to science and art and reorganizing and drilling their army, so as to be able to protect their country against all nations. The Eastern boundaries of Egypt were well protected by strong fortresses. This is but natural, because on the East, the Semitic or white races reigned, and no doubt they were unfriendly to the Egyptians Moors, or "black" people, because they had expelled the Shepherd or "white" Kings from their land. Now, when the Egyptians had attained "in that Age" to the highest degree of intelligence and wisdom, and were possessed of the greatest human power, God deemed it wise to make His own Infinite wisdom and power felt over that of human wisdom and power, by using Moses as an instrument to knock at the door of the Egyptian government and ask for the release of the enslaved Jews. Moses did not appear in Egypt by any human authority, or power, but by the authority and the power of God, for it would have been useless for not only Moses, but for any nation or number of nations to approach Egypt with hostile intentions, without God, because Egypt with her wisdom and power had the world at her mercy. There it required God with His immeasurable wisdom and power to overcome the wisdom and power of the Egyptians Moors. The evidence of God's power was displayed to the "Pharaoh Meneptah," who is generally conceded to be the "Pharaoh of the Exodus," by His, "God's" instruments, Moses and Aaron who were to appear before the Pharaoh and cast down their rods which turned to serpents (Exodus 7:10). When they had cast down their rods before Pharaoh, and they turned to serpents, Pharaoh called the wise men, or magicians of Egypt with their enchantments, and they cast down their rods which also became serpents (Exodus 7:11,12).

This was the performing of two miracles, one by God's power, and one by human power. This vying with God, though only for an instance of time is what no Caucasian man has had the power to do since his creation. But, however, God, in order to demonstrate His supreme power, caused the serpents transformed from the rods of Moses and Aaron to swallow the serpents transformed from the rods of Pharaoh's or Egypt's wise men (Exodus 7-12). This rod and serpent incident was the beginning of a series of plague miracles (Exodus 7; 8; 9; 10), which wrecked the Egyptians' Moors or black man's kingdom, and also destroyed that great power which he had over all other nations and released the Jews from slavery. **The black man's power, as the first power among the nations had now begun to decay, and as the black race began to die, as a power among nations, the white race began to rise to where it had never been before, but this was 2,500 years after the black man had worked out all the problems of civilization.**

In reading Revelation, 13: 11, John, describes:

"I behold another beast coming up out of the earth and he had two horns, like lamb's, and he spoke as a dragon." Now, to some, the foregoing vision of John was this very country, the United States of America, before this country was discovered and named, some would claim the two horns interpreted to be the two great political parties that have done so much to corrupt Government and misrule its people from their infancy to the present day. The American Government spoke like a dragon when it permitted slavery to exist, especially when its Constitution says "That ALL MEN WERE BORN FREE AND EQUAL......" Now, concerning the theory of this nations, their rise and fall, that is the will and the work of God to be of Divine help to the people of Israel in representation of the "EAGLE" to which the "CHURCH EXIST" Rev. 12:6-14 So, since it is true that the black man is the father of civilization, it is just as true that the white man is now at the helm, and the big "I AM" of the civilized world.

But the fact remains that he took his civilization and his position after the black man had created it, and passed it from the stage of action, just as the white man must do at God's own appointed time, to make room for some other race, such as the yellow race, Chinese or Japanese so as the Federal Government Census point out by the year 2030. David, the Psalmist, said: "Egypt was the land of the black nation—Ham not Shem, the Caucasian man," and he further said that the Tabernacles which were the houses and dwellings from the lowest to the King's palaces were Ham's — (Psalms, 106: 22 105:23, 27; 78:51). It is easy to understand why the black man is not identified with his Egyptian Moors; that reason is seldom honestly and earnestly sought for. The reason is—that the historians, with a very few exceptions, write from a prejudiced standpoint, together with the fact that they do not give credit to the Old Testament, if indeed, they study it at all, especially that part of it which is the most ancient, and beyond all shadow of a doubt the first and only TRUE account of the origin of mankind it is easy to understand.

It is impossible for God to forget that the black man and his land (Egypt) was the cradle of rescue that rocked and nursed the Son of God in his first two years of life, when Herod's decree to destroy all children less than two years of age was issued. It was known that the decree was issued for the express and only purpose of destroying the infant Christ, but God chose Egypt, the land of the black nation, as a haven of rest and safety during the life of the displeased and would-be infant murderer, Herod. (Matt., 2)

This might be the origin of that old, old saying, "Blood is thicker than water," for Jesus in going into Egypt, went among black women and men, who were the founders of the tribe from which he sprang. When God in His infinite wisdom, His great love, justice and mercy, and at His own appointed time, summons mankind to take his rightful place in the wavering human line to be rewarded for that smallest of virtues, in proportion as he for the greatest of virtues, will say to the black nation, who will be found heading the line, **"Well done, you good and faithful servants, the reason to live, you are, My instrument, The Father of Civilization."**

CHAPTER II

The Love For Life

The meaning and purpose of life isn't all that easy to figure out. What does it mean to have meaning and purpose? How do you determine what that is? Do you determine your own meaning? Can you combine what you think is your own purpose with the purpose that someone else might have for you?

"Everyone who is called by My name, And whom I have created for My glory,

Whom I have formed, even whom I have made," (<u>Isaiah 43:7</u>).

According to the Bible, our purpose, the reason we are here, is for God's glory. In other words, our purpose is to serve <u>God</u>, honor and worship him, to proclaim his greatness, and to accomplish his will. This is what glorifies him. Therefore, in this we find that God has given us a reason for our existence, a meaning for our existence. We were created by him, according to his desire, and our lives are to be lived for him so that we might accomplish what he has for us to do. When we trust the one who has made us, who works all things after the counsel of his will (<u>Ephesians 1:11</u>), then we are able to love a life of purpose. How the particulars of that purpose are expressed is up to the individual. What if our lives are difficult and things go wrong? Are our failures and hardships for the glory of God, too? Yes, they are.

We often thank God and praise his name when things go well, but we often turn our backs on him and complain when things are difficult. Sometimes our appreciation and trust in God becomes conditioned on how well things are going for us. Ultimately, this is self-centered immaturity. Even though things can go wrong in our lives, the ultimate reason we are here is to serve for the purpose to glorify God -- even through the difficulties. We do this by seeking him and trusting him through difficult times. Within this attempt to glorify God -- in all things -- we can then determine the particular meaning of our love for life that God has for us specifically. In Christianity, we are free to pursue God in all areas of our lives. For example, we are free to glorify God by being a doctor, a lawyer, a mechanic, a housewife, a father, a mother, a minister, an accountant and more. If the ultimate goal in life is to bring glory to God then we can do that by being the best at what we do in the various callings of life. So, as the Bible says, "...whatever you do, do all to the glory of God," (1 Cor. 10:31). There are those will not like this. There are those who will deny that God has made us. For them, they want to determine their own purpose. They must decide for themselves what is meaningful to them. They want their independence. They want to proclaim what is good and bad in their own hearts, and determine their purpose based on their desires. But the problem is that this becomes self-serving. When we do what we think is right in our own eyes, we often make mistakes -- especially when we deny God. When a child says "I want, I want, I want," he is showing his immaturity and self-centeredness. Adults become other-centered as is demonstrated by the sacrifices involved in parenthood and marriage. As we grow older, we realize the value in considering the interests of others. "Do not *merely* look out for your own personal interests, but also for the interests of others," (Phil. 2:4). In this, we learn that purpose is best defined not by selfish desires but by the ability to love life and consider others more important. This carries over to receiving a purpose from God. If we are selfish and want to determine our own purpose, then how does that truly love Life? After all, if love is other-centered then shouldn't we love God, center our lives on him, and humble ourselves before him in his wisdom and trust what he desires for us? Think about it. He knows infinitely more than we do, and by trusting him we can discover the ultimate purpose of our lives. It makes sense.

Moralism is simply doing what is good for goodness sake. An atheist can do that, but for those who claim to be Christians our purpose is not our own glory. The meaning of our lives is to bring glory to God (Isa. 43:7). Unbelievers do not know God. Therefore, they can only be moralistic in their self-determination of meaning and purpose. That is, they have no objective moral standard that exists outside of themselves and so they have no way of knowing what their ultimate purpose really is. They will then, at best, adopt a kind of moralism, a goodness that is relative to the preferences and situation and live a kind of conditional love. In that way, they cannot know what real goodness is. And without knowing what truly is good, how can they truly have a good purpose in their lives? The right thing to do is bring glory to God because there is no one greater who is worthy of trust, adoration, and worship. Therefore, for the   Christian, we are to live to bring glory to God. How we do that is through seeking and study of his word, the Bible, so that we might better know what he has for us. See! the bible says...God foreknew all things long before the foundation of the world because he planned these things; God set the things of the world up according to his purpose and plan, which means good and evil. And the one thing God knew is that man had to be tested as his greatest project, we all were destined to be tested. Our first point of testing would be who we are and what our purpose on earth is and Adam being first man (after the Pre-Adamite world) he was first in line for this powerful testing of man's will. God put in order all the things that would be man's first point of attack, in doing so God gave man the good of all things first (Heaven) over the evil of all things (Hell), this in the manner of the perfect world before the fall. This also accounts to that in the perfect world one difference between the Kingdom of God and the kingdom Devil is that God presents Heaven from beginning to end (Alpha & Omega) and Devils kingdom don't exist, but because of the fall the difference is now that Devil presents Heaven first Hell last and God presents Hell first and Heaven last.

So it was vitally important for God to give image (Identity) first because the greatest destruction to a man's life is not knowing **"Who he is" or "What his purpose is"** on this earth, that is the greatest tragedy to **"MAN."** It does not matter how much money you have, what position you carry in life, how much power and authority you posses, if you don't know who you are as a man you are dangerous in a world of death and destruction and you will easily add to this world of death and destruction. Here is what we missed in this matter of God's purpose and plan in our lives, we keep thinking it is dominion or ruler ship with an iron fist over the earth and in all that we are too have, we have been chasing **"Power over Purpose", believing that our purpose here on earth was and is to obtain power, man was created to rule and dominate the earth...yes, but the first thing given to man was not power, it was image, see God knew that power would be in trouble if image was not in order, why because the fall of man would give devil the power over man to redirect man's image of God to the image of the world**. This is the reason why we will never be satisfied with having more money, you don't need money first **"MEN,"** money is attracted to the right self image, money moves toward a man who knows who he is and when you know who you are you don't seek to obtain power by way of having more money. Solomon says, **in (Eccl. 5:10-12) He who loves money will not be satisfied with money, nor he who loves abundance with its income. This too is a waste. When good things increase, those who consume them increase. So what is the advantage to their owners except to look on? The sleep of the working man is pleasant, whether he eats little or much; but the full stomach of the rich man does not allow him to sleep.** You can easily tell when a man has a low self image; he has an inferiority complex, he looks to scheme or scam for things, so he needs to accumulate things to build up his insecurity that's why he has a lot of material things because he has no self image and his identity is defined by what he has. A man who loses everything and still smile is a righteous man, a righteous man don't need things to be of value, because a righteous man give value too things. So God put in place the work, given Adam responsibility to go along with His Image because image needs a place of existence and when God places something in us it must be express in the world, so as Adam is placed in the Garden, Gods image was there to be express.

We must know and understand that your work is not your job. When God place Adam in the Garden He gave Adam dominion over it and everything in it, so noted everything including the woman. Now everything means five different kingdoms on earth, **1.) Fish....2.), Birds....3.), Livestock....4.), All the Earth, plants, trees and grass....and 5.), everything that creeps on the ground (insects).** Now your job is your skill, a policeman, a fireman and a postman that's one skill, your work is the gift that you were born with. For instants when you go to your job you enter in an atmosphere of people all operating on one skill and in that skill you put in an 8 hour day and you has a human person over you called a boss. When you do the wrong thing on this job you are fired from this job. When you are fired from this job you **"MAN"**....go home to your place of rest and you are met at the door by your wife and she says "hello honey I have work for you to do, I need you to cut the grass, I need you to fix the roof, I need you to too wash the car, I need you to clean the basement. Now take your job and your work at home and line it up to the Garden Adam was given dominion over and see which one is identical to the Garden before the fall, **"THE HOME"** because in the home you **"MAN,"** have dominion over the work which is your gift you were born with, your job which is your skill and have a human boss over you are not identified to with the Garden. God did not place any one over Adam, this is why we men naturally hate to be ruled over because we were not created to be ruled, but created to dominate. Only after the fall is when God place in the Garden a Guardian Angel to protect the tree of life in the east of the Garden and this Angel was used to fire Adam and Eve from the Garden..."**A BOSS"**....see the Identity. **"YOUR JOB IS NOT THE WORK GOD GAVE YOU MEN"** It is important to know the different so you can know your purpose, other than that you will be stuck in a place that you hate. The one thing that we have to understand as men is simply knowing GOD did not create man to rule man, GOD never said to man have dominion over man, it was the woman, the animal kingdoms and the earth that was given to us rule and regulate.

This is why we as men have many issues on the job and other control environments simply because we were not made to be controlled but too control all things on earth, by way of GOD's Kingdom plan and purpose in our life on this place called earth. We must know and understand that we only can rule our own GOD given territory, which then we collaborate that portion of our dominion over the earth. To rule over or have dominion over this place such as the earth means all that the earth gives off in trouble, difficulty, problems, issues, pain and agony is for man to put in check or in perspective that these things be resolve as they come, not man singular, man collectively Paul says— **"We should no longer be children, tossed to and fro and carried about with every wind of doctrine." He added, "But, speaking the truth in love, may we grow up in all things into Him who is the head— Christ— from whom the whole body, joined and knit together by what every joint supplies, according to the effective working by which every part does its share, causes growth of the body for the edifying of itself in love"** (Eph. 14-16). Our dominion was not given to us singular it was given to us as a whole, in a collaborative collective bargaining reason and relationship as men in Christ. We are given a limited time to carry out GOD's purpose here on earth and the time that you think you have is not set up for your foolishness or ill gotten ways. What you may believe to be correct could very well be a waste of time given to do the purpose that you don't have a clue to which you must carry out. Many men believe there job is there purpose or just doing a good deed holds as your purpose, your purpose is that what you are born with, and do you know what's in you? Do you know GOD well enough to know what you're here for? Do you understand the struggle you've come through? Do you understand struggle at all? Or more so **"DO YOU KNOW GOD?"** No matter whom you are or where you come from every one of us has been given unique purpose we all were born with. GOD created every one of us with this unique gift to make an impact on earth that it would be a lasting impact for generations to come, your impact as man on earth is to maintain the set stage Christ set for us from the foundations of the earth as Paul says— "Just as He chose us in Him before the foundation of the world, that we would be holy and blameless before Him" (Eph. 4).

Long before the world was established GOD chose us, we men, were given the position to govern this earth in accord to GODs purpose and plan place in us, not according to our ways and means. We are given the position to carry out the very assignment that is uniquely place in us that we specifically exercise our skill set for the very purpose of being a threat too devils kingdom, given devil no breathing room to take charge of our families, friends and neighbors. We should act as an legion of warriors daily simply because of devils legion of demons that stay on the war path twenty-four hours a day as he spoke to GOD when ask in Job— " The Lord ask Satan, "where have you come from? "Satan answered the Lord, "from wandering all over the earth." Job 1:7; other Hebrew writings speaks extensively in saying— "looking to devour man all over the earth," in other words we men are under constant attack to remove us from whom GOD placed on this earth to be "Manager" of this place called earth, we are to maintain our families, our communities our environment that all that is in it live with honor, respect and glory first too GOD and then by way of his image we live. We cannot continue this easy path of destruction that many of you are on, given devil an open door policy to do what he wish in your life, leading you away from being men and developing your choices to be like **"WOMEN"** through a **"LIE"** of a chosen homosexual lifestyle. Given Satan the keys to death over your life when GOD through His son Christ Jesus upon dying on the cross and descending down into hell and taking the keys of death from the hands of   Satan and making death a footstool under His feet. We no longer have to fall under death simply because death is under our feet as Paul says— **"even when we were dead in our transgressions, made us alive together with Christ (by grace you have been saved), and raised us up with Him, and seated us with Him in the heavenly places in Christ Jesus....** (Eph. 2:6-7). In a world of trouble and chaos, in which we as men brought about such foolishness by way of allowing ourselves too be tossed to and fro like the wind, when we have no business in such turmoil being the very ones given dominion over the earth. We have a God given duty to act in accord to the will of God, in His image to stand as the foundation of the family place in our care under our instruction by way of one wife and respectful children.

Our nature is too follow the life of God as we were created for, not too follow our on desires but the that which represent God and that which represent God is that which we were made in, his **"IMAGE."** God's image represents a unified body called the **"Trinity"** a bond that will never be broken under no circumstances. This is the same standard God holds man too under no circumstance man should be apart from God, under no circumstances should man be apart from a wife, under no circumstances should man be apart from his children, this is not what God has given us dominion to become, independent men from our families. We are the bond to hold us together in Christ; we hold the most important position on earth in which we are held to a strict account to manage this earth accordingly as Christ by way of the instructions of the Holy Spirit. Too many men are given up their position as men in a world you were given strict instructions to manage, along with the knowledge, understanding and wisdom to do so, how do you give up such a position over the **"WORLD."** It is simple when you have no idea of what you are, who you are or why you even exist, you have no position to hold on too, How can you hold to a position you never knew you posses. This is why the bible shows us Gods purpose and plan will go on with us or without us. The word of God tells us that God will supply our needs and all that we receive is nothing but supplies, the problem behind that is we take the supplies and use the supplies to maintain ourselves on earth but our treasures and rewards are stored in Heaven. We are taking our supplies and using them in the manner of our treasures and rewards and Christ says we already then have received our reward on earth that we were to receive in Heaven. The Greatest tool the Devil use against us as men of God is independency, if Satan can cause us to be independent from God he then can have his way, and fallen astray means fallen prey to **"Death."**

Having dominion over the earth comes with our will to choose outside of God's control of that area of our life, so in doing so we don't give God the experience of what we experience at the moment of our lives in our experiences How? By not choosing him to intervene in our experiences. How do you choose? By prayer and the spoken word (Sanctification), many times we think God test us for discipline reason in what we do and in many cases that's true but in other cases God test us men not on what we do but for what we know. This why we as men must always depend on God, case in point, radio test their systems for dependency on their back up in case something goes wrong same with TV Station, in other words God test us in two forms "A manner of Discipline" and " a manner of Dependency" or Faith. Who you love? Do you love the things that God gave or do you love God for what He has given you, that **"Thing."** These are the many of issues we face as men in going forth in God, one problem to note we have as men of God is many of you continue to try to prove your point in your life, instead of proving Gods point in your life, and you stop trying to prove your point and seek God's point then the righteous point will be made. We all need to understand our relationship with God and how that relationship dictates the man we will, or will not, be, we must learn how to discern the voice of the Lord through the instructions of the Holy Spirit and how to respond to that small still voice. It is that very voice of love, mercy and kindness that we can somehow find ourselves at odds with when we are tempted, we as men need convictions that doesn't come from other men, we need convictions from hearing the voice of the Lord. They come from having a holy fear of God and knowing in your heart of hearts his will for you. Convictions allow a man to steady his walk in order to stay on the narrow road that leads to life, to be able to hear the voice of the Lord, discern his will in your life, and to act upon it in a way that brings him glory is everything you need to be a true man. **OFF AND ON,** As Paul says to the Ephesians, "Praise be to God and father of our lord Jesus Christ, Who has blessed us in the heavenly realms with every spiritual blessing in Christ. For he chose us in him before the creation of the world to be holy and blameless in the sight of Him, (Eph. 1:3-4), then he added, "You were taught, with regard to your former way of life, to put off your old self, which is being corrupted by its deceitful desires; to be made new in the attitude of your minds; and to put on the attitude of your minds; and to put on the new self, created to be like God in His true righteousness and holiness"— Eph. 4:21-24. How can we—creatures who are physical and spiritual and fallen in our sin—obey this verse?

How can we—creatures who are physical and spiritual and fallen in our sin—obey this verse? How can we triumph over our sin and our flesh to perform this profoundly spiritual act? More to the point the bible, if you and I have a hard enough time trying to obey this verse, how can immature men accomplish this? Simple every immature unrighteous man will have the same origin as every one of the righteous spiritual victories. To rise above the temptations of the world you must set the mind on the things of the Spirit. Scripture teaches us to put to death those thoughts and desires that are of the earthly nature and to begin to show evidence of our new spiritual nature that is "being renewed in knowledge in the image of God. Put to death, therefore, whatever belongs to your earthly nature: sexual immorality, impurity, lust, evil desires and greed, which is idolatry, because of these; the wrath of God is coming? You used to walk in these ways, in the life you once lived, but now you must rid yourselves of all such things as anger, rage, malice, slander, and filthy language from your lips. Do not lie to each other, since you have taken off your old self with its practices and have put on the new self, which is being renewed in knowledge in the image of God. Here there is no Greek or Jew, circumcised or uncircumcised, barbarian, Scythian, slave or free, but Christ is all, and is in all. Therefore, as God's chosen people, holy and dearly loved, clothe yourselves with compassion, kindness, humility, gentleness and patience. Bear with each other and forgive whatever grievances you may have against one another, forgive as the Lord forgave you, and over all these virtues put on love, which binds them all together in perfect unity. (Col. 3:5-14). We have been made in God's image, we have the amazing privilege of being spiritual beings, just as God is a spiritual being, the responsibility that comes with that privilege (privilege and together) is that we are called to pursue spiritual growth. We are called to become ever more "like God in true righteousness and holiness." This pursuit is the essence of honorable manhood, even honorable young manhood. That's a daunting project, isn't it? Does it seem impossible? As impossible, I don't know, a camel squeezing through the eye of a needle? If that's how you see it, you're on the right track. Not only that, but you're in the right place to be able to communicate this truth accurately to the young men, for our Savior told us that, "with man this is impossible, but with God all things are possible" (Matt 19:26).

Here's the challenge men need to understand, like Adam, we are required to be perfectly blameless and completely holy in our obedience to God. The problem, of course, is that none of us ever do this perfectly, as James said, "We all stumble in many ways" (James 3:2), so if we are sure to fail from time to time, yet God calls us to be perfectly holy, what does it mean to walk as a man before God? It means that we must put our trust completely in the finished work of Jesus Christ, who alone can make us holy and pure. It means that when we stumble and fall short of the glory of God we do two things, First, we return to the Lord and ask him for forgiveness, genuinely repentant yet confident that this specific sin we just committed was a sin Christ died to forgive. Second, we pick ourselves up again and keep going, continually seeking to obey God by the power of his grace. This is the basis of all repentance: turning away from our sin and in our love of God heading in the opposite direction, back to him again and again. This is where our degree of familiarity and our current experience with God's word becomes crucial, Through the Bible we learn and are reminded of what God commands of us, and we recall the power and love and grace he offers us for both obedience and forgiveness. This means we should be continually growing in our knowledge of God through his word, the Psalmist certainly got it right when he wrote, "How can a young man keep his way pure? By living according to your Word. I seek you with all my heart; do not let me stray from your commands, I have hidden your Word in my heart that I might not sin against you" (Psalm 119:9-11).

Man then, is a spiritual creatures, we are made in God's image, we are called by his grace to live in perfect holiness before him, and when we fail we can look to Christ for forgiveness and fresh grace. How then can we measure our progress, our success? How can we know we are becoming more like God in righteousness and true holiness? Actually, it's not that difficult, as we growth can be readily seen in the virtues, or character traits, that rise to the surface, what virtues should we aim for? What do we want our sons to be like? Let's start with a definition of manhood that is currently popular in much of western culture. According to this definition, a "real man" can be described something like this: Muscular and athletic, Never overweight, Definitely not an acne sufferer, A rugged   individualist who answers only to himself, a person who is tolerant of everyone and everything, because there are no absolutes in his life, only opinions, open to many views of morality, truth, and right and wrong, a ladies' man, with the emphasis on the plural, even if his choice in "ladies" is another man, Basically deserving of anything he might want or desire, focused on being (or at least appearing to be) wealthy, smart, accepted, talented, liked, and admired. Is this the kind of man you hope your boy will become? Are these the "virtues" you want to see manifested in his life? I don't think so. In Galatians 5:19-21 Paul describes the nature to lead us into "sexual immorality, impurity and witchcraft; hatred, discord, jealousy, fits of rage, selfish ambition, dissensions, factions and envy; drunkenness, orgies, and the like." Paul then contrasts these detestable things of our sinful nature with the fruit of the Spirit of God in Gal. 5;22-23, "but the fruit of the Spirit is love, joy, peace, patience, kindness, goodness, faithfulness, gentleness and self-control." I believe we can distill from Scripture six virtues to use as benchmarks and goals, things we can hold onto, measures, evaluate, and work to improve as we mature. It is not my intention to make an airtight case for these six being the only possible choices; certainly there are other virtues that can be identified in Scripture. My goal here — especially as you prepare to talk with your son—is to keep it simple by providing a biblically solid list that is easy to remember and will point your son in right direction.

A biblical description of a real man is a follows. A real man is: Humble, Courageous, Morally pure, Faithful, Selfless, and Self-Controlled. How well do these terms line up with that first set of bullet point—the worldly view of a man? Not a lot of overlap, is there? Where are the self-centeredness, self-seeking, and self-glorification that the world continually emphasizes? Where are the themes of consumption and indulgence? Where is the sense of entitlement? In their place, we see a striking emphasis on looking outward. The second set of bullet points describe a man who takes the attitude of a servant toward others, whose life is focused not on self-exaltation but on glorifying God with his life. The world's version of a man essentially sees others as raw material for his own gratification and glorification, the true man, on the other hand, according to God's definition, seeks to love his neighbor and to consider others as better than himself. **The Virtues of Men,** these virtues are spiritual fruit, closely and directly associated with being like God in true righteousness and holiness, the more we become like God, the more these virtues will be evident in us. For each virtue there is a short definition and a few verses for emphasis and elaboration, paying close attention to these virtues will help you set your sights on exactly where you want to lead your son. **Humility,** to pursue humility means choosing to accept the fact that your knowledge and abilities are limited, and in light of that, you are regularly seeking help and graciously receiving advice and correction. This one is esteem: he who is humble and contrite in spirit, and trembles at my word (Isa. 66:2), all of you, clothe yourselves with humility toward one another, because, God opposes the proud but gives grace to the humble (1 Peter 5:8), Humility and the fear of the Lord bring wealth and honor and life (Prov. 22:4). **Courage,** to pursue courage means choosing to do what is right despite the opposition of others or of your own desires (often the more difficult enemy to fight), be on your guard; stand firm in the faith; be men of courage; be strong (1 Corinth. 16:13), so keep up your courage, men, for I have faith in God that it will happen just as he told me (Acts 27:25), Act will courage, and may the Lord be with who do well, (2 Chronicles 19:11),

Purity, to pursue moral purity means choosing to live by the highest moral principles in both speech and physical relations, despite your own desires to do otherwise, and despite any external pressure to compromise. How can a young man keep his way pure? By living according to your word (Psalm 119:9) treat younger men as brothers, older women as mothers, and younger women as sisters, with absolute purity (1 Tim. 5:1-2). Set an example for the believers in speech, in life, in love, in faith and in purity (1 Tim. 4:12), do not be hasty in the laying on of hands, and do not share in the sins of others, keep yourself pure (1 Tim. 5:22). **Faithfulness.,** to pursue faithfulness means acting in integrity, keeping your words, and doing what is right before God, with fortitude and without complaint, because you trust God to give you the ability to complete all he has given you to do, so then, men ought to regard us as servants of Christ and as those entrusted with the secret things of God. Now it is required that those who have given a trust must prove faithful (1 Corinthians 4:1-2), Love the LORD, all his saints! The LORD preserves the faithful, but the proud he pays back in full. Be strong and take heart, all you who hope in the LORD (Psalm 31:23-24), A faithful man will be richly blessed (Prov. 28:20). Selflessness, to pursue selflessness means placing the well-being of others before your own needs and desires. An unfriendly man pursues selfish ends; he defies all sound judgment (Prov. 18:1), Do nothing out of selfish ambition or vain conceit, but in humility consider others better than yourselves, Each of you should look not only to your own interest, but also to the interests of others (Philippians 2:2-4). For where you have envy and selfish ambition, there you find disorder and every evil practice (James 3:16). **Self-control,** to pursue self-control means to live according to the Spirit of God, choosing to glorify God with our lives and deny the sinful nature when tempted to do otherwise. Be self-controlled and alert, your enemy the devil prowls around like a roaring lion looking for someone to devour (1 Peter 5:8), Like a city whose walls are broken down is a man who lacks self-control (Prov. 25:28). But the fruit of the Spirit is love, joy, peace, patience, kindness, goodness, faithfulness, gentleness and self-control, against such things there is no law (Galatians 5:22-23).

We all need help, when society settles on a false definition of what is good and desirable in a man, the streets become full of males who have never grown into Biblical manhood. Guys like these might look cool, but morally they may be little more than children, what a sad and traffic things that so many boys today fall into this trap and never get out! They buy into the world's definition of manhood and end up going to their graves morally stunted. The externals of chasing this worldly definition of manhood—things like sexual conquests, shiny never qualify anyone for true manhood. Your son doesn't have to become a man like that, he has you to help him, and you have Christ, the Word of God, and fellow believers to help you. The truth is that we all need help, being a man is a daunting task, impossible on your own, to become more like Christ in true righteousness and holiness, a man's mind must be renewed and his heart must be regenerated. In short, your son needs divine intervention, and you must remind him of his dependence on God and the regenerating work of Jesus Christ. For your son to be the man that he was created to be requires full and complete reliance on Jesus Christ, It is in this God–given, God-empowered virtues that your talk with your son should be wrapped. I guarantee these are not character traits or choices that have been discussed with your son at a public school, They are rarely seen on television or in the movies, if you want to be sure your son has an understanding of what it means to be a man, you will most likely need to be the one to tell him. In any event, you are far and away the best one to tell him. The bibles says— as a man thinks within himself, so he is….(Prov. 23:7), if you think yourself to be less than a man you are, if anyone put the thought of any death disease in your thinking and you accept it than it will be, if you think you can't stand up against life's issues, than it will be, if you think you can't handle life's struggles, then you can't, if you think you can't handle life's difficulties then you won't, if you think you can't handle life's problems then so it will be. What was the purpose of all that struggle you came thru life for?

What did you experience all that pain in life for? You weren't born without reason! God did not give purpose to all of creation to follow and live by and not give you a purpose. When Eve committed the sin in the Garden of Eden the bible says Adam was right there with her as she committed the sin, but the bible also says when God entered into the Garden through his son Christ Jesus (Lord) it was not Eve that was sought after, it was Adam that was sought after why? Simply because Adam was given the authority over the earth and everything in it. It was Adam that was given the instructions to carry out the duties in which the garden was to be cared for and past down to Eve to do the same has her husband. When the things of this earth goes against us, when stuff fall apart in the families, when the community become disarray, when the church is not making an impact on the community as it should, when the kids are out of order, when the wife no longer set her eyes for you only, when the house is no longer a home. Who is the blame Devil? A defeated **FOE**? The bible says— **"How you have fallen from heaven, morning star, son of the dawn! You have been cast down to the dawn! You have been cast down to the earth, you who once laid low the nations!......Those who see you stare at you, they ponder your fate: " Is this the man who shook the earth and made kingdoms tremble, the man who made the world a wilderness, who overthrow its cities and would not let his captives go home?** (Isaiah 14:12 –23). He is a **"DEFEATED FOE"** so you can't put nothing on devil men, all things is based on our will to choose, that's the freedom the bible is clear about a man's responsibility to exercise spiritual maturity and spiritual leadership. Of course, this spiritual maturity takes time to develop, and it is a gift of the Holy Spirit working within the life of the believer, the disciplines of the Christian life, including prayer and serious Bible study, are among the means God uses to mold a boy into a man and to bring spiritual maturity into life of one who charged to lead a wife and family. Embrace maturity, as you may have heard it said: Maturity does not come with age, but with the acceptance of responsibility, if we are going to grow as men, we have to take full responsibility for our lives-blaming no one; owning our decisions; and deciding to grow and change-no matter what has come our way. Gen. 3:12 says— "after sinning, Adam said to God, "The woman whom you have given to me, she gave me of the tree and I ate."

Notice how Adam dealt with his being caught in sin, 1. **He blamed his wife- "the woman you gave me…" 2. He blamed God: "….the woman you gave me…" 3. As a result of Adam blaming her, she followed his example and blamed the devil when she said to God, "The serpent deceived me and I ate."** This spiritual leadership is central to the Christian vision of marriage and family life, a man's spiritual leadership is not a matter of dictatorial power, but of firm and credible spiritual leadership and   influence. A man must be ready to lead his wife and his children in a way that will honor God, demonstrate godliness, inculcate Christian character, and lead his family to desire Christ and to seek God's glory. Spiritual maturity is a mark of true Christian manhood, and a spiritual immature man is, in at least this crucial sense, spiritually just a boy. **Personal maturity** sufficient to be responsible husbands and father true masculinity is not a matter of exhibiting supposedly masculine characteristics devoid of the context of responsibility. In the Bible, a man is called to fulfill his role as husband and father, unless granted the gift of celibacy for gospel service, the Christian boy is aim for marriage and fatherhood.

This is assuredly a counter-cultural assertion, but the role of husband and father is central to manhood. Marriage is unparalleled in its effect on men, as it channels their energies and directs their responsibilities to the devoted covenant of marriage and the grace-filled civilization of the family. They must aspire to be the kind of man a Christian woman would gladly marry and Christian will trust, respect and obey. A real man knows how to earn, manage and respect money, a Christian man understands the danger that comes from the loves money and fulfills his responsibility as a Christian steward. Of course, men come in many sizes and demonstrate different levels of physical strength, but common to all men is a maturity, through which a man demonstrates his masculinity by movement, confidence and strength. A man must be ready to put his physical strength on line to protect his wife and children and to fulfill his God-assigned tasks, a boy must be taught to channel his developing strength and emerging size into a self-consciousness of responsibility, recognizing that that adult strength is to be combined with adult responsibility and true maturity. **Sexual maturity** sufficient to marry and fulfill God's purposes even as the society celebrates sex in every form and at every age, the true Christian man practices sexual integrity, avoiding pornography, fornication, all forms of sexual promiscuity and corruption. He understands the danger of lust, but rejoices in the sexual capacity and reproductive power God has put within him, committing himself to find a wife, and earn her love, trust and admiration — and eventually to win her hand in marriage. It's critical that men respect this incredible gift, and to protect this gift until, within the context of the holy marriage, they are able to fulfill this gift, love their wives and look to God's gift of children. Male sexuality separated from the context and integrity of marriage is an explosive and dangerous reality. **Ethical maturity** sufficient to make responsible decisions, to be a man is to make decisions; one of the fundamental tasks of leadership is decision-making. The indecisiveness of so many contemporary males is evidence of a stunted manhood. Of course, a man does not rush to a decision without thought, consideration or care, but a man does put himself on the line in making a decision — and making it stick. This requires an extension of moral responsibility into mature ethical decision-making that brings glory to God, is faithful to God's Word and is open to moral scrutiny. A real man knows how to make a decision and live with its consequences — even if that means that he must later acknowledge that he has learned by making a bad decision, and then by making the appropriate correction.

Worldview maturity sufficient to understand what is really important. An inversion of values marks our postmodern age, and the predicament of modern manhood is made all the more perplexing by the fact that many men lack the capacity of consistent national and International thinking. For the Christian, this is doubly tragic, for our Christian discipleship must be demonstrated in the development of Biblical principle. The Kingdom of GOD, man must understand how to interpret and evaluate issues across the board of politics, economics, morality, entertainment, education and a seemingly endless list of other entities. A man seeks to demonstrate emotional strength, consistency and steadfastness; he must be able to relate to his wife, his children, his peers, his colleagues and a host of others in a way that demonstrates respect, understanding and appropriate love for his family. This will not be learned by entering into the secret world experienced by many male adolescents. **Maturity sufficient,** to make a contribution to society while the home is an essential and inescapable focus of a man's responsibility, he is also called out of the home into the workplace and the larger world as a witness, and as one who will make a contribution to the common good. God has created human beings as social creatures, and even though our ultimate citizenship is in the Kingdom of Heaven, we must also fulfill our citizenship on earth. **Character maturity, sufficient to demonstrate courage under fire.** The literature of manhood is replete with stories of courage, bravery and audacity. At least, that's the way it used to be. Now, with manhood both minimalized and marginalized by cultural elite, ideological subversion and media confusion, we must recapture a commitment to courage that is translated into the real-life challenges faced by the Christian man. At times, this quality of courage is demonstrated when a man risks his own life in defense of others, especially his wife and children, but also anyone who is in need of rescue. More often, this courage is demonstrated in taking a stand under hostile fire, refusing to succumb to the temptation of silence and standing as a model and example to others, who will then be encouraged to stand their own ground. In these days, biblical manhood requires great courage.

The prevailing ideologies and worldviews of this age are inherently hostile to Christian truth and are corrosive to Christian faithfulness. It takes great courage for a man to devote himself unreservedly to his wife. It takes great courage to say no to what this culture insists is the rightful pleasures and delights of the flesh. It takes courage to serve as a godly husband and father, to raise children in the nurture and admonition of the Lord. It takes courage to maintain personal integrity in a world that devalues the truth, disparages God's Word, and promises self-fulfillment and happiness only through the assertion of undiluted personal autonomy. A man's true confidence is rooted in the wells of courage, and courage is evidence of character. In the end, a man's character is revealed in the crucible of everyday challenges. For most men, life will also bring moments when extraordinary courage will be required, if he is to remain faithful and true. **Biblical maturity sufficient to lead at some level in the church,** takes a close look at many churches will reveal that a central problem is the lack of biblical maturity among the men of the congregation and a lack of biblical knowledge that leaves men ill equipped and completely unprepared to exercise spiritual leadership. While God has appointed specific officers for his church — men who are specially gifted and publicly called — every man should fulfill some leadership responsibility within the life of the congregation. For some men, this may mean a less public role of leadership than is the case with others. In any event, a man should be able to teach *someone,* and to lead in *some* ministry, translating his personal discipleship into the fulfillment of a godly call. There is a role of leadership for every man in every church, whether that role is public or private, large or small, official or unofficial. A man should know how to pray before others, to present the Gospel and to stand in the gap where a leadership need is apparent. The position of the husband in the home and his related responsibilities are quite clearly defined in principle in Ephesians 5:22, 28-31. "Wives submit yourselves to your own husbands, as to the Lord. For the husband is head of the wife, even as Christ is head of the church; and he is the savior of the body. Therefore as the church is subject to Christ, so let wives be to their own husbands in everything.

Husbands love your wife as Christ also loved the church and gave himself for it . . . So ought men to love their wives as their own bodies. He who loves his wife loves himself. For no man ever yet hated his own flesh but nourishes and cherishes it, even as the Lord the church . . . For this cause shall a man leave his father and mother and shal.1 be joined unto his wife, and they two shall be one flesh". It is impossible to completely deal with the responsibilities of the husband in a book alone. Let us start with some scriptures that deal with the husband as head of the house. Genesis 3:16, says in part "her desire shall be to man". Then Eph. 5:23, "husband is head of the wife"; then I Tim. 2:11-12, "She shall have no dominion over a man," the only responsibility of the husband is to be HEAD of the house. The head does not mean master as in a master-slave relationship, nor does it mean a relationship like a general to a private in the army and the Head does not mean standing on top of the home. It is a partnership where one is the leader, guide, and director. Not to make that a husband should make any decisions WITHOUT consulting or considering his wife and her wishes.

CHAPTER III

Eternal Life

RENOVATION **OF THE EARTH,** Immediately after the destruction of Satan and his armies, John says— I saw a Great White Throne and Him that sat on it, from whose face the Earth and the Heavens (atmosphere of the earth) fled away; and there was no place for them. Rev. 20:11. John then Describes the Judgment of the "Great White Throne," and then adds—I saw a New Heaven and a New Earth; for the first heaven and the first earth will pass away; and there was no more sea. Rev. 21:1 of such a change in the earth we are not ignorant, but John does not tell us how it is too come to pass. But the Apostle Peter does. But the heavens and the earth which are now, by the same word are kept in store, reserved to Fire against the Day of Perdition of Ungodly Men. (The Great White Throne Judgment)— The Day of the Lord will come as a Thief in the Night; in which the Heavens shall pass away with a Great Noise, and the Elements shall be Melt with Fervent heat, the Earth also and the works that are therein shall be Burned up. Nevertheless we according to His promise, (Isa. 65:17; 66:22) look for a New Heaven and a New Earth, wherein dwells righteousness. 2 Peter. 3:7-13. it is clear that Peter is referring to the same event as John, for he says it is to be at the Day of Judgment and Perdition of Ungodly Men, and that is the "Great White Throne Judgment" of the Wicked Dead. A surface reading of the above passage would lead one to believe that the Earth as a planet and the sidereal heavens (the Stars in the Universe) are to be destroyed by fire and pass away.

But a careful study of the Scriptures shows us that this is not so, that what is to happen is, that this present earth and the atmosphere surrounding it, is to be Renovated by fire, so that its exterior surface can be completely changed and all that sin has brought into existence, such as thorns and thistles, disease germs, insects pests, etc, shall be destroyed, and the atmosphere purified and forever freed from evil spirits and destructive agencies. That this is the correct view of the passage is clear from peter's words in 5 and 6. "By the word of God the Heavens were of Old, and the earth standing out of the water and in the water, whereby the world that then was, being overflowed with water, PERISHED. The world that the Apostle was   referring to here was not the Antediluvian World" that was changed by the "Flood," but to the Primeval World," mentioned in Gen. 1:1, and which was made waste and void by a Flood that completely submerged it. The Apostle Peter divides the history of the earth into three periods. The period before the Earth was made "formless and void" or the Primeval Earth, which he calls the world that then was, the present period which he calls the heavens and earth which are Now, and in which there has been no great change since the restoration of the earth described in Gen. 1:3-2:1; and the New Heaven and Earth which is yet future. 2 Pet. 3:5-7, 13. Now as the frame work of the Primeval Earth was not destroyed by its "Watery Bath," so the frame work of the present Earth is not to be destroyed by its "Baptism of Fire." This is confirmed by the Apostle's use of the Greek word "Cosmos" which means the land surface, the inhabitableness of the earth, and not earth as a planet. It is the exterior surface of the earth then that is to melt with Fervent Heat and the "Works therein Burnt Up. The intense heat will cause the gases in the atmosphere to explode, which the Apostle describes as the heavens (the atmosphere), passing away with great noise. The results will be the destruction of all animals and vegetable life, and the alteration of the destruction of all animals and vegetable life, the alteration of the earth's surface. The Greek work "Parerchomai," translated pass away. Does not mean termination of existence or annihilation, but means to pass from one condition to another. The Apostle Paul in his letter to Titus, (Titus 3:5), speaking of the "Regeneration" of men, use the same word that   Jesus used when, in Matt. 19:28, He promised His Disciples that in the Regeneration," that in the New Earth they shall sit on "Twelve Thrones" judging the twelve Tribes of Israel. Now no one supposes that the Regeneration of a man is his Annihilation. It is simply a renewing Process in which he is brought back to the condition of man spiritually as before the Fall.

The word Restitution in Acts 3:21 mean the same thing. The dissolving of which Peter speaks, (2 Pet. 3:11), is the same word Jesus used when he said of the colt—"loose him and let him go. The teaching of the scriptures is that Creation is at present in a State of Captivity, waiting to be loose from the bondage that sin has caused. Rom. 8:19-23. As to the "Departing as a Scroll" of the heavens, and the "Flying Away" of the earth and heavens, of which John speaks, Rev. (6:14; 20:11), a total disappearance of all the material worlds is not at all the idea, for he tells us that afterwards he saw—the New Jerusalem coming out of Heaven, and nations living and walking in the Light of it and the Kings of the Earth bringing their Glory and Honor in it. Rev. 21:2, 24. The Holy Spirit by Solomon said, "One generation passes away, another generation comes, but Earth abides Forever. Eccl. 1:4. It is specifically promise that the Meek shall inherit the Earth, (Matt. 5:5), and the Children of Israel shall dwell in it forever, (Isa. 60:21; 66:22), and if God's people are to inhabit it forever, it must exist forever. It is clear then that this Earth as a Planet is not to be annihilated, but that it is to be clean and purified by Fire and made fit for home of those peoples and nations that are to occupy it after its renovation. This Earth that has been consecrated by the presence of the Son of God, where the costliest sacrifice that the Universe could furnish was offered up on Calvary to redeem a race, for which God has a great future, is too sacred a place too ever be blotted out or cease to exist, for it is the most cherished orb in the mind of God of all His great creation. The New Heaven and The New Earth, with the renovation of the Earth by Fire, time does not end and Eternity begin, for we read in the New Testament of a "Perfect Kingdom," that Christ shall surrender to the Father, so that God can be "All in All" 1 Cor. 15:24-28. A Kingdom in which—At the name of Jesus, every knee shall bow, of things in Heaven, and things in Earth, and things Under the Earth, and that every tongue shall confess Jesus Christ IS LORD. Phil. 2:9-11. This describes a Kingdom in which all things Celestial, Terrestrial and Infernal are to be subject to the Son of Man. Now the perfect Kingdom cannot be Millennial Kingdom, for that, as we have seen, ends in Apostasy and Rebellion. It must be therefore mean another Kingdom on the other side of the Millennial Kingdom, and as there is to be no other Kingdom between the Millennial Kingdom and Renovation of the Earth by Fire, it must mean a Kingdom that is to follow the Renovation of the Earth by Fire, and that Kingdom of the New Heaven and the New Earth, rightly dividing the world, the perfect Kingdom.

And as the duration of God's Covenant with Israel was extended in Deut. 7:9 to a thousand generation or 33,000 years, we have an intimation that the Dispensation of the Fullness of Times will last for at least that length of time. Let us look at some of the characteristics of that Age or Dispensation. There will be no sin, All the power of evil will have been expelled from the earth and imprisoned in the Lake of Fire forever. The atmosphere of the New Earth will afford no lurking place for disease germs, for there shall be no more sickness or death, and the health will be preserved by the use of leaves of the "Tree of Life." the heavens will not robe themselves in angry tempests and somber blackness, nor flash with the thunder bolt of Divine wrath, nor cast plagues of hail on the earth, nor cause devouring floods of water or destructive wind storms. It may be in that day, a mist shall go up from the earth and water the whole face of the ground as in Eden, for we read that there shall be— No More Sea, not that there shall not be large bodies of water, for the river that flows through the street of the New City must have an outlet, but that there shall not be no great oceans. The Earth shall also put on its Edenic beauty and glory. There shall no longer be thorns and thistles, no parasites or destructive insects, and labor shall be a delight. No serpent shall hiss among its flowers, nor savage beast lie in ambush to destroy and devour. Its sod shall not be heap over newly made graves, nor its soil moistened with tears of sorrow and shame, or saturated with human blood in fratricidal strife (killing one's own brother). The meek shall inherit the earth, and from the north to the south and from the east to west, it shall blossom like the rose and be clothed with the verdure of Paradise Restored. But there is not only to be a New Heaven and a New Earth there is to be a New City. This city is the place Jesus said he was going back to heaven and prepare for His bride the Church. John 14:2-4. it is just such a place that we should expect the Divine Architect to design and build. The   description of it is surpassingly grand. It is of Celestial origin. It is not Heaven itself, for it comes down out of Heaven. Nor mortal hands are employed in its construction. It will take up it abode on the New Earth, and we see in this why this present Earth will have to be renovated by fire, and why there shall be no more sea, 1500 square miles, and would reach from Maine to Florida, and from the Atlantic Coast line 600 miles to the West of the Mississippi River. In other words would occupy more the one-half of the United States.

We are told that the length and breadth and the height of it are equal. This does not necessarily imply that it is a Cube, for there is another geometrical figure that has equal dimensions, and that is a Pyramid. This is probable form, for a wall 144 cubits, or 216 feet thick, could not support a wall 1500 miles high, and a wall that high would hide the pyramidal part of the City from view. The 144 cubits (Rev. 21:17) then must refer to the height of the wall. In this wall are 12 gates, 3 on each side, each gate of one Pearl and these gates are never closed. The wall itself is of Jasper, and the foundations are garnished with all manner of precious stones. The foundations contain the names of the Twelve Apostles of the Lamb, and over the gates are the names of the Twelve Tribes of Israel. What a magnificent spectacle such a city must present from a distance with its pyramidal top surmounted by the light of the Glory of God. For the city has no need of the sun, neither of the moon, to shine in it, for the Glory of God did lighten it, and the lamb is the Light Thereof. Rev. 21:23. "And the gates of it shall be No Night There. Rev. 21:25. This refers to the City only, and not to the outlying parts of the Earth, for there will be day and night wherever the light of the City does not reach. The Pyramidal part of the City will doubtless be in the center of the City, and probably not occupy over one-half of the surface area, leaving the remainder to be divided up into boulevards and Avenues with numerous parks and residential sections. We are told that the City itself is of pure Gold, like to clear glass. Rev. 21:18, if this refers to the houses and homes of inhabitants, then redeemed are to live in palaces of Transparent Gold, and the streets redeemed are to live in palaces of transparent Gold, and the streets are to be the same material. Rev. 21: 18, 21. We cannot imagine a City with such dwellings and streets to be unclean or lack beauty. The streets are to be lined with trees, as are also the banks of a wonderful river. These trees are not mere shade trees, but beautiful Fruit Trees, called the Tree of Life, that bear Twelve Kinds of Fruit, a different kind each month. The first of these trees is for Overcomers Only. To him that overcomes will I give to eat of the Tree of Life, which is in the midst of the Paradise of God" Rev. 2:7. The leaves of the trees are for the Healing of the Nations what shall occupy the New Earth. Not that there will be any sickness, but to preserve them in health, as Adam would have been preserved in health if he had eaten of the Tree of Life in the Garden of Eden. Gen. 3:22-24. The wonderful river is called the River of the Water of Life, because of its Life giving properties. Earthly streams have their source in some mountain spring, but the "River of Life" has its source in the Throne of God.

Rev. 22:1. Somewhere on that Pyramidal Mountain in the center of the City, probably on its summit, will rest The Throne of God, from under the seat of which shall flow down in cascades, from terrace to terrace, trace the crystal stream that feed that wonderful "River of Life." Whoever heard of an earthly city without some place of worship, be it heathen or Christian, but the wonderful thing about the New Jerusalem is that it has no Temple. Why need a Temple when the object of worship is present for the "Lord God Almighty and the Lamb Are the Temple of It." In fact the whole City itself will be a Temple. Then the Tabernacle of God shall be with men, and He will dwell with them, and they shall be His People, and God Himself shall be with them, and be their God. And God shall wipe away all tears from their God. And God shall wipe away all tears from their eyes; and there shall be no more death, neither sorrow, nor crying, neither shall there be any more pain; for the "Former Thing Are Passed Away." Rev. 21:3, 4. This means that Heaven shall have come down to Earth, and that this earth will become the Residence of God. Outside the walls of this beautiful City, spread over the surface of the New Earth," nations shall dwell, whose kings shall bring their glory and honor into it, but nothing that will defile or work abomination shall ever enter in through those "Gates of Pearls" for there will be no sin on that New Earth. Rev. 21:24-27. Who Are to the Happy Inhabitants of this New Earth? Where did the people who inhabited the earth after the Flood come from? They were the lineal descendants of Noah, how did they escape the flood? They were saved in an Ark which God Provided Gen. 6:13-16. Shall not God then during the "Renovation of the Earth by fire, in some manner, not as yet revealed, take off righteous representatives of the Millennial nations that He purpose to save, and when the earth is again fit to be the abode of men, place them back on the New Earth, that they may increase and multiply and replenish it, as Adam (Gen. 1:27, 28), Noah (Gen. 9:1), were told multiply and replenish the present earth. If God could take off Elijah for the purpose of sending him back again to herald the Second Coming of the Lord, surely God can take off representative men from the nations and put them back again on the New Earth to repopulate it. If this is not God's plan then we have one type in the Scriptures that has no antitype, for Noah's Ark, which is a type, has no antitype unless it be this.

It is clear from the Scriptures that God does not purpose to create a new race for the New Earth. His promise as to Israel is that the descendants of Abraham shall inherit this earth for a "thousand generation," or 33,000; now this is not possible unless they are transplanted to the New Earth. And this just what God has promised. "For as the New Heaven and the New Earth, which I will make, shall remain before Me, says the Lord, so shall Your Seed and Your Name Remain. Isa. 66:22. It seems clear from the presence of the Tree of Life in the Garden of Eden, that God intended the human race to populate the Earth, and when it became too thickly populated, to use the surplus population to colonize other spheres. Our "Solar System" is only in its infancy. The earth is the only one of its planets as yet habitable. Where are the inhabitants for the other planets to come from? Think that the planets of our Solar System, and the planets of other Solar System, of which the stars are the suns, were made simply to adorn the heavens for our little earth? God does not plan things on a Small Scale, and it magnifies His power and wisdom to believe that He created man in His own likeness, a created being higher than the angels and gifted with the power of Procreation, that He might by means of him populate the Universe. That magnifies the Scheme of Redemption; you think God gave His Son to die on Calvary just to redeem a few million of the human race? Why He could have blotted them out, as He probably did the Pre-Adamite race, and created a new race, and Satan would have laughed because he had the second time blocked God's plan for the peopling of this earth. No God will not permit Satan to block His plan for peopling this earth with a Sinless   Human Race. The death of Christ was not merely to redeem a few million of the human race, but to redeem the Earth, and the Race itself from the curse of sin, and the dominion of Satan. The Apostle James tells us that we only the "First Fruits" of His Creatures. James 1:18. What then must the Harvest Be? The Universe is young yet, we are only in the beginning of things, for "of the increase of His government and peace there shall be no END." Isa. 9:7. When this Earth shall have gone through its "Baptism of Fire," and shall be again fit for the occupancy of man, the representatives of the "Saved Nation" (Rev. 21: 24) will be men and women in whom no taint of sin will remain, and who cannot therefore impart it to their offspring, who will be like the offspring of Adam and Eve would have been if they had not sinned. This magnifies the whole scheme redemption, and justifies God in the creation of the human race.

The Great Abdication, the "Millennial Age" and the "Perfect Age," between which the Earth is Renovated by Fire, make up the "Age of Ages," which period is called the Kingdom of the Son of Man. At the close the "Age of Ages" shall have put down all rule and all authority and power. For He must reign till He has put all enemies under his feet, " then Christ as the Son of Man , shall surrender the Kingdom to God, that God may be All in All, 1 Cor. 15:24-28. This is known as The Great Abdication (renounce the Throne); there have been many abdications of Thrones in the world's history, but none like this. Thrones have been abdicated various reasons. Some have been forced, others voluntary. Some on the account of physical ailment, or to secure some particular successor. But Christ will not abdicate for any of these reasons. He will abdicate because He has Finished the Work That Was Given Him to Do as the Son of Man. He will not   surrender His human Nature, but His title "Son of Man" will merge back into that of "Son of God" so that the Divine Godhead shall thereafter act in its Unity, and God shall be 'All in All." This will end what we understand by Time. Then Eternity will begin, which will be divided up into the Ages of the Ages. Of its end there is no hint just " **THE SIGN OF THE TIME."**

CHAPTER IV

Who Has Power

&

Authority Over Life

"So do not be afraid of them, for there is nothing concealed that will not be disclosed, or hidden that will not be made known.

What I tell you in the dark, speak in the daylight; what is whispered in your ear, proclaim from the roofs. Do not be afraid of those who kill the body but cannot kill the soul.

Rather, be afraid of the One who can destroy both soul and body in hell. Are not two sparrows sold for a penny? Yet not one of them will fall to the ground outside your Father's care.

And even the very hairs of your head are all numbered. So don't be afraid; you are worth more than many sparrows.

"Whoever acknowledges me before others, I will also acknowledge before my Father in heaven. But whoever disowns me before others, I will disown before my Father in heaven. Matt. 10:28-32.

We're living in dangerous days! No doubt that our generation is experiencing the birth pangs of the tribulation time that Jesus said would precede His return to earth (Matthew 24). During that time of great judgment, Satan will unleash perhaps his greatest onslaught of killing, stealing, and destroying ever (Revelation 12:12)! God has given us everything we need to live successfully in this hour! Jesus Christ has provided a redemption of which the benefits far exceed the effects of Adam's fall! When Jesus said, "All authority has been given unto me in heaven and in earth," and then said, "go you therefore."(Matthew 28:18-20), He literally gave us His own authority to deal with Satan, our enemy and every act of stealing, killing, and destroying that he would unleash against the body of Christ. Authority is delegated power. A person's authority exceeds his personal strength! The police officer directing traffic in the middle of the street is wearing a badge on his uniform that puts the power of the government supporting that badge behind the hand that he holds up! A large truck could easily crush him in the middle of the busy street, but because the driver understands the power of the badge, he quickly yields his will and submits the power of his large vehicle to the authority of the badge! As a believer, you have been given the authority of the kingdom of heaven; the actual authority that Jesus has over Satan to deal with him and his onslaughts in your life! God knew that you needed a weapon of defense and offence when He redeemed you and left you in a fallen world with a malevolent enemy that seeks to harm you and your family. This authority enables you to send Satan on the run before he harms your family. Let's examine this authority for just a moment. Remember that God gave the first man Adam, authority over the earth and its fullness when he was created (Genesis 1:26-28). Psalm 8:4-6 reveals that God made man just a bit lower than Himself and gave man His authority over the world. In quoting this verse, the author of Hebrews reveals that this authority has been stopped and that now the earth is not under man's control. (Hebrews 2:6-8) Satan mentioned that the authority of the kingdoms of the world was delivered to him and that he could give that authority to Jesus if He would bow down to him (Luke 4:4-6). This was a legitimate temptation.

When Adam sinned, he broke fellowship with God and the entire human race. He also gave away the authority that God originally gave to him at creation. Jesus knew that He would legally reclaim the lost authority of man in His death and resurrection! Colossians 2:15 reveals that Jesus ".disarmed principalities and powers, making a public spectacle of them, triumphing over them in it (the cross)." Of what he disarmed them, you may ask. Jesus disarmed them of the authority they received from Adam when he sinned, and then He gave that authority back to the church! When Jesus was raised from the dead, He was seated beside the Father "far above all principalities and power and might and dominion, and every name that is named, not only in this age but also in the age to come. And He put all things under His feet, and gave Him to be head over all things to the church, which is His body, the fullness of Him who fills all in all" (Ephesians 1:21-23). In the light of Jesus' position in heaven, God "raised us up together, and made us sit together in the heavenly places in Christ Jesus" (Ephesians 2:6)! What that means is that we share the very authority that Jesus has over Satanic forces seeking to harm us! Look at it this way; Jesus didn't defeat the devil for Himself, He already had authority over him (See Luke 10:17-19) He defeated Satan as a man ("the second Adam, or the Last Adam, 1 Corinthians 15:45, 47) representing the human race so that we too could exercise   authority over our adversary who "walks about as a roaring lion, seeking whom he may devour" (1 Peter 5:8-9).

Christians have access to the "badge" of authority in the use of the name of Jesus! Jesus has given us the unqualified use of His name in His absence. His NAME represents His person, His position, His seating, and His authority! "If you ask (demand) anything in my name, I will do it" (John 14:14). Jesus' name will accomplish everything that He can without Him personally being present! "Most assuredly, I say to you, he who believes in me, the works that I do will he do also; and greater works than these he will do, because I go to the Father" (John 14:12). His name is above every name! Every demon force must bow to the name JESUS! (See Philippians 2:9-11). Ok, let's make this practical now, and bring these truths down into daily life and put "shoe leather" on them. Every time you or your family are attacked with sickness, disease, or physical weakness of any kind, rise up in the NAME OF JESUS and command Satan to take his hands off of you or your family member! You have been given AUTHORITY that is far greater than your natural strength. To do nothing about it, or to whine and complain about how bad things are will only give Satan control over you! That would be like the police officer laying down in the street and crying   because a vehicle refused to obey his instructions! He has to enforce the law and sometimes that means forcing people to submit to what they know is right! Satan is the same way. If you lie down and do nothing when attacked, He will dominate you. That's what most believers do   today! When confronted with financial lack, oppression, depression, fear, weakness, failure, or anything else that steals, kills, and destroys, RISE UP IN THE NAME OF JESUS AND   COMMAND SATAN'S POWER TO BE BROKEN OVER YOUR LIFE AND FAMILY! No one has more authority in your life and family than you do! I personally "take charge" of my life spiritually each morning by submitting myself afresh to Jesus' Lordship over me, and then I command Satan and his forces to BACK OFF and leave my family and church alone in the NAME OF THE LORD JESUS CHRIST! Don't wait until a crisis arises. ASSERT YOUR RIGHTS AND PRIVILEDGES IN CHRIST JESUS AGAINST SATAN TODAY AND SEND HIM ON THE RUN, BEFORE HE TRIES TO HINDER YOUR LIFE OR YOUR FAMILY! Remember that we overcome by "the blood of the Lamb," and by the "word of our testimony," (Rev. 12:11) and by the use of the Name of Jesus. Because of Jesus, we are already made "more than conquerors" (Romans 8:37)

Part II
Stop
Killing
Me Black Man

CHAPTER V

The Love of Death

&

Destruction

"Terrorism" **Defined:**

the calculated use of violence (or threat of violence) against civilians in order to attain goals that are political or religious or ideological in nature; this is done through intimidation or coercion or instilling fear....Between 1824 and 1951 there were over 300 events classified as "White Race Riots" in which entire white communities turned on and destroyed entire Black communities and murdered Blacks in mass. There were 26 such major events and hundreds of smaller ones in major cities and towns across the US during the summer of 1919 alone. This period has been tagged by historians as *The Red Summer of 1919*, because many of the events happened from May to October of that year and the blood of their victims literally painted the streets of America. That year, tens of thousands of Black Americans were killed, maimed and 375,000 were made refugees, though never being given refugee status, all for economic, social, political and other reasons both real and imaginary. They even killed Blacks for recreation activities in rural areas in events called "Friday Night Boot Burnings" *(the burning of a Black man at a stake or bonfire)* or "Picnic" *(a slang term for pick a nigger for lynching}* Lynching became a common weekly event to kill the monotony of rural life. It was not uncommon for whites to eat, drink, dance and sing church songs as they created a sadistic festive atmosphere, while their victims suffered from torture.

White men, men women and children all participated in what was best described by Ida B. Wells-Barnett as "An orgy of murder and mayhem." Many times whites massacred based purely on perceived notions and paranoia, such as in Helena and Phillips, Arkansas in 1919. The white landowners envisioned a Black union meeting was an organized uprising and Negros was planning to kill whites in mass at some future date. The reality was the Black farmers, sharecroppers' and farm workers held a meeting after forming a union to demand a fair accounting from the whites on their sharecropper accounts, after being cheated for years. They were armed and had no intention of disarming because of what happened in East St. Louis in 1917. When the sheriff attempted to serve a warrant as a pretext to investigating the union meeting, a gun fight ensued and the sheriff was killed and other whites were wounded. The white landowners feeling depraved feared a great financial loss and with bloodlust in their hearts over their dead friends, they hunted Blacks like dogs through the woods and killed 25 to 125 Blacks early in the manhunt. The best official death count came to 854. No one knows the actual number because of how the bodies were treated and disposed of. They wounded many hundreds more and caused every Black citizen in every surrounding county to flee for their lives too. Today, Blacks in Helena and Phillips County are now planning to seek reparations for their ordeal. They made it perfectly clear, if you had a Black skin, you had two choices. You were either dead, or moving. Floaters *(dead bodies in the river)* were popping up daily for weeks after the riot was over. Again the National Guard was called and again they joined the white rioters. During the Red Summer Riots of 1919, a common characteristic in every case was the Black American was alone and helpless when it came to protecting or defending himself and his community. Many had assumed then, as we do now, that our government is supposed to protect us from invaders from within our borders and from foreign nations. THEY WERE DEAD WRONG! After studying White Race Riots, collecting relics', investigating reports, reading hundreds of newspaper reports and first hand testimonials, I have determined based on the circumstances that Black Americans must protect and defend themselves from their countrymen. This assumption is based on the following findings:

1. No government military branches where there to protect them. The National Guardsmen would join the   rioters and shoot Blacks too. Many just looked the other way because they hated "niggers" too. Or they came in time to put out fires, mostly in the white sections of town, or white owned rental properties in the Black neighborhood only.

2. The Police joined or aided the white rioters. Deputized white Policemen burned out women and children and used them for target practice, for sport and wager, as they threw them back into the flames that they   attempted to escape. Police disarmed Blacks and stud back to let the white rioters do what they wanted without fear of justice or the law.

In the Tulsa Race Riot of 1921, police flew airplanes and dropped nitroglycerin and dynamite on 600 Black businesses, burned 1500 homes and destroyed a 35 square block area of the Black community of Tulsa also known as the Greenwood District. It was so prosperous it was nationally known as Black Wall Street. The riot was intended to put Blacks back in their place. The American Legion and the KKK and white military veterans and fraternal organizations offered their services in tracking down and killing Blacks. They often lead in mobs and initiated the riddling of many of their Black victims. ROTC cadets assisted in hunting, dragging, burning, killing and maiming during post war times. In all cases not one white person was ever convicted of murdering a Black person regardless of how horrible their crimes. Hate was part of the fabric of white American society. They protected their "Supreme" status at all cost. Blacks had no value and no souls. Blacks had no rights. Blacks weren't people and in political discussions Blacks existence was referred to as the "negro question". To the average whites ALL Blacks were niggers. In 1920 2 out of 10 whites in America were members of the KKK. Blacks were de-humanized so whites could commit any heinous act without guilt and with impunity. It's hard to kill one of Gods human beings, but easy to kill a thousand niggers.

In Detroit 1943, 4300 Federal Troops wounded 2500 Blacks after the last of the great white race riots. Police, local whites, National Guard and Federal troops turned on Black Detroit. Blacks were beaten openly in public by literally thousands of whites chasing and beating them while police searched and disarmed them to make them easy prey. The Detroit Police Department participated in many murders and freely participated in mayhem towards Blacks. Every Black person in sight was searched and even their pocket knives were removed. Then they were left to the white rioters who in turn, maimed or murdered a totally defenseless victim. Police were rerouting Blacks in motor vehicles to dead ends where white rioters where waiting to beat and murder them. Many Blacks had placed their faith in the hands of Police for protection, only to have that trust betrayed, and their lives exterminated. The methods of murders in white race riots were similar in each case, which included but not limited to: Lynching, burning, castration, stoning, bullet riddling, just plain shot, dragged in the street, drowned, beat, punched, hit with assorted objects, heads split with an axe and more than can be imagined by any ungodly person. It was common for a single Black victim to incur all of the above forms of punishment from his fellow American. Bodies have been subjected to this type of treatment with as many as 100 plus individual whites to 1 Black victim. Many bodies were reported to be punished for hours after the victim was already dead. They became merchants of the macabre as they cut up the victims' bodies into parts for resale as, souvenirs, mementos, and mantle pieces. Black victims had hearts, lips, ears, fingers, spleen, liver, lungs, intestines, penis, hands, heads, scrotum and all other body parts and even the Black fetus was not spared. A poor Black pregnant woman Mary Turner in Georgia had her unborn child cut from her womb as she burned at the stake. While she was inflamed a white man stepped from the crowd, slit her stomach with his pocket knife, and when the fetus fell to the ground, he stomped it and said "One less nigger". Thousands of curbside spectators slapped their knees as they laughed in amusement. Mary's crime: She had disputed the word of a white man that falsely accused her husband of murdering a white man in a dispute over money owed him by the white man. A shoot out ensued. The white man died in what otherwise was a fair fight. For her protest after they lynched her husband before her eyes, they tied her to a tree, poured gas on her, oil and set her on fire.

After she writhed silently in the flames in defiance of the "mad and hungry dogs", she was doused a second time as white children danced and chanted in song and rhyme. In the terms of property damage. Whole city blocks in Black communities have been burned to the ground and many Black property owners had to abandon their homes while running for dear life, with only the clothes on their backs, if they were lucky enough to live through home invasions, hails of bullets and fire bombs during the initial attack. Many of the aftermaths resemble ground zero of a nuclear blast. In the Tulsa riot, you could see from one end of the Black business district, and see clear to the opposite side without the obstruction of your view by any physical objects. The land was totally leveled for 3 miles through Black Tulsa. White race riots caused over 375,000 Blacks to leave the South and Southern Border States, and flood the Northern States. Even in states as far north as Minnesota were still unsafe as riots became more of a characteristic in northern cities, than in the South. Many as refugees with only the shirts on their backs. This period in history is called "The Great Migration" In the summer of 1919 the riots. White Race Riots occurred mainly in the northern states, while individual lynching's were more common in rural areas in the South. Blacks involved in other riots between 1917 and 1923, recalled the horrors of the East St. Louis race riot, in which 250 to 700 Blacks (or more) were massacred in the most gruesome fashion, dared to fight back. They decided it was better to fight a good losing battle, than to die like rats in a barrel. Blacks armed themselves in mass in order to defend themselves. Not to initiate attacks on whites. Blacks across the nation refused to disarm themselves when requested to do so by law enforcement and conveyed to whites, that they are ready to maintain and use arms, whether the whites liked it or not, if threatened. If such an event occurred today, Blacks would be sufficiently unarmed because of past and current gun control laws that were enacted specifically to disarm them.

We would be virtually caught like deer in the head lights. The most recognized massacre of Blacks in mass in our time, came to light in the movie "Rosewood" in which the small Black township in Florida was destroyed and an estimated 150 Blacks were killed as the township was literally wiped from the face of the earth in 1923, and more recently revealed Tulsa Race Riot of 1921, where an estimated 300 to 3000 Blacks were killed in just 12 hours. Over 7800 were left homeless and over 17,000 fled for their lives by foot, train, automobile and horseback or any other means of transportation. Whites used crop duster airplanes nitroglycerin and dynamite to bomb and destroy over 600 Black businesses in a 35 square block area. This was the real "Oklahoma City Bombing" Survivors of the Tulsa so called riot, that was really a massacres, have successfully gained reparations for the murderous and destructive acts of white Americans upon their ancestors. As bad as each of these events were none before or since then equal the level of barbarity, butchery and savagery committed by white Christian men women and children, at 11: o'clock am, on July 2nd 1917. Congress in its great wisdom decided that the circumstances surrounding The East St. Louis Massacre of 1917 were to be preserved for future generations to deal with. The effect that resulted was, that all of the hundreds to thousands of whites that murdered between 250 and 700 unarmed Black men, women and children in the most despicable ways ever chronicled in American history, none would ever be brought to justice to pay for their crimes. The criminals are all so old today they are either already dead or dying. That includes Black survivors of the holocaust. The act of hiding the details of the horrific event also deprived Black America of justice. It is pure and simple premeditated case of Justice Denied." Adolph Hitler was a corporal in the Austrian army on this day in 1917, and even he shunned white America for its level of savagery. As an historical foot note, some historians feel the Germans got their plan for their "final solution" to the Jewish problem from America's treatment of Blacks between 1914 and 1935. The newspaper accounts of the East St. Louis Massacre and other lynching's and white race riots were widely circulated in the French, English and German press. Nazi Germans realized that if the entire dominant community is against a minority or unpopular members of that community, after sufficient vilification of the minority or unpopular group, the dominant group can do what they want no matter how horrible the punishment.

It will mirror public opinion and thereby be justified. The Nazi cause was also the same as White Supremacy in the United States. The 65th Congress left the circumstances evolving around this event for future generations to discuss. That generation is ours. The East St. Louis Massacre of 1917 is exhibit. A" evidence for reparations for past atrocities against Black Americans. Not as former slaves, but as human beings and free citizens of the United States. "It is the ultimate end of unchecked American Racism. From 1999 to 2009, among those aged 15 to 34 years, there were 106,271 homicides, 85% (89,887) among men and 49% (52,265) among black men. One major and hotly debated issue is firearms. Specifically, 81% (85,643) of all homicides were due to firearms, including 91% (47,513) among black men. Homicide is, far and away, the leading cause of death of young black men. In stark contrast, accidents are, far and away, the leading cause of death among young nonblack men and women of all races and ethnicities. Black men are 6 times more likely to die as the result of and 7 times more likely to commit murder than their white counterparts. One eighth of the population is black, but one half of all homicide victims are black. Their reduced life expectancy of more than 6 years would be improved more from eliminating homicide than abolishing any other causes of death except cardiovascular disease or cancer. The rate at which Blacks killed Blacks in 1994 was 876 times greater, and the rate at which they killed Whites was 164 times greater, than the rate at which Whites killed Blacks. Whites were twice as likely to be killed by Blacks as by Hispanics. Blacks were twice as likely as Hispanics and 71 times as likely as Whites to kill members of their own race. One quarter of the nation's homicides were committed by the 0.7% of the population who were Black men between the ages of 18-24. If there were no Blacks or Hispanics in the US at all, our homicide rate might be as low as North Dakota, or 0.2 per 100,000 populations, which is 1/49th of its all time high of 9.8 in 1991. Such an extraordinary homicide rate cost this putative Christian nation an extra 24,209 American lives in 1991 alone, and 800,000 during the 20th Century--a loss of life three times greater than all American WWII battle deaths and 200 times greater than the loss attributable to "terrorism" by Muslims. Black crime in America is real, it's present, it's ongoing, it's pervasive--and it would be far easier to correct than any war on Muslim Terrorists. So why is it not corrected?

Why do we instead go to war against 1.2 billion Muslims in the world, when we didn't lift a finger to protect the 50 million WHITE Christians in Russia from the Bolshevists? Why do we continue to imprison 6% of black men in the US for trivial crimes, and possibly crimes that they didn't even commit, while NOT imprisoning the black murderers? For the last two decades, the affirmative action hires in our justice system have FAILED to even prosecute a third of all the murderers in the country, leaving up to a quarter of a million murderers free to murder again--and again. Whites, who commit only 5% of these murders, represent 30% of our prison population, so it's not White murderers who aren't being imprisoned--it's mostly black murderers. What is the plan here? What better way to create resentment by Blacks against Whites than to falsely imprison Blacks who didn't commit crimes while not imprisoning Black murderers?

Blacks murder six Whites in the US every day.

Young black men are 175 more likely than White women to be murderers and 145 times more likely to be   murdered. Blacks & Hispanics in America caused an additional 22,374 murders in 1995.

Genocide of American Whites by blacks and Hispanics:

> Proven by the US government statistics.
>
> Ignored by the "news" media.
>
> Took 200 times as many American lives in the 20th Century than Osama bin Ladin.
>
> Homicides per 100,000 populations by race:
>
> Whites = 0.7.
>
> Hispanics = 27.
>
> Blacks = 52.

The large variation in the homicide rate from state to state is due almost exclusively to the higher proportion of blacks and Hispanics in some states coupled with their higher propensity to commit murder, particularly in Washington, DC. People in states like North Dakota, Vermont, Iowa, and South Dakota are up to 1/100th as likely to be murdered as people in states like Louisiana, California, New York and Maryland and 1/355th as likely as people in Washington, DC.

But the percentage of the population who are blacks and Hispanics in North Dakota is 1/33rd that of California and 1/58th that of Washington, DC. Every one of the states with a high percentage of blacks and Hispanics has a high murder rate, including California whose low percentage of blacks is made up for by a high percentage of Hispanics. The result is that Hispanics alone are a mortal risk to Californians which exceeds the risk of dying from tobacco smoke by two to three times. If the entire country had had a homicide rate equivalent to North Dakota's rate of 0.2 per 100,000 population in 1995, rather than 22,895 homicides that year, there would have been only 526 homicides, saving 22,369 American lives. Such a rate over the last half century would have saved more than 893,000 American lives, making multiculturalism an expensive proposition for American Whites. But perhaps it's a boon to blacks and Hispanics who may have killed each other in even greater numbers if Whites hadn't been around to organize their society for them. Had the homicide rate that year been equivalent to Maryland's, 8,672 more Americans would have died, and had it been equivalent to Washington's, 164,776 more Americans would have died. It's likely that Washington's rate would have been even higher had it not been for the 28% of the population there who are Whites. North Dakota is living proof that White Americans living free of multiculturalism and race mixing could have an even more stable society than Norway or Japan. This low murder rate in 1995 was not a fluke, because North Dakota's rate has remained the same or even declined over the last two decades. This is not a new situation for states like Maine, Iowa, Montana, New Hampshire, and South Dakota, either, because they have consistently had the lowest murder rates. And they also haven't been bombarded with multiculturalism, miscegenation and the influx of blacks and Hispanics like the high crime states have.

These rates are also equivalent to countries like Singapore, the Slovak Republic, England, Wales, Cyprus and Japan, which also stand as living proof that low crime rates aren't a distant and impossible dream. Whites who have not been bombarded with miscegenation manage to keep their homicide rate at around 0.7 per 100,000 population, whereas blacks who live in White societies commit 52 homicides per 100,000 blacks and Hispanics commit 27 homicides per 100,000 Hispanics. This is one of the most heinous examples of the chronic media bias faced by White Americans each day. This inexplicable and chronic propensity to cover up almost every crime perpetrated on, legal system bias against, justice system discrimination against, and to belittle every action by, the White Christian man must stop, now. The mainstream media openly supports "hate crime legislation" which would effectively benefit every American citizen except the White Christian man. It focuses on one crime committed by White American men against one black felon James Byrd for an entire year, while ignoring almost 2,500 black Americans who murder Whites every year. The rate at which black Americans murder Whites is 8.2 per 100,000 Blacks, a rate higher than the murder rate of all but a few countries, and more than 8 times higher than countries like the Czech Republic, Japan, Cyprus, England, Wales, the Slovak Republic, and Singapore. The likelihood that a Black American will murder a White American is 65 times greater than the likelihood that a citizen of Singapore will be murdered at all. Black men between the ages of 18-24 commit murder at a rate 175 greater than that of White and Hispanic women (and Hispanic women commit 85% of those murders). Between 1991 and 1994 they murdered at a rate of 350 per 100,000 populations, but were murdered at a rate of "only" 175 per 100,000. The other half of their murder victims were mostly White men. If such a high murder rate were to be sustained over the next 75 years (the average life expectancy in the US), then more than a quarter of all blacks in the US would have murdered someone (not including multiple murders by one person). Thanks to affirmative action putting the most incompetent bureaucrats in charge of our justice system (which reduced our "clearance rate" for murder to an all time low) more than a quarter of a million murderers have never been brought to justice just in the last 30 years, and most of them are black.

Of the 25,869 homicides in the US in 1993 reported by the National Center for Health Statistics, only 16,297 were resolved, leaving 9,572 murderers Scot free, to murder again, and again. We have 3.7 unresolved homicides per 100,000 populations which is more unresolved murders per capita than the above countries have total murders per capita. Had the US homicide rate remained at its already high rate before the first of our 22,000 gun control laws was passed in 1965, there would have been 550,000 fewer homicides since then. The problem is not ownership of firearms by Whites--it is ownership of firearms by blacks who cannot be entrusted with that right--not in Africa, and not in the US. While Whites are a significant percentage of the victims of the ownership of firearms by blacks, blacks are an even bigger percentage. While Whites are a significant percentage of the convictions which were based solely on the existence of these 22,000 unconstitutional gun control laws (and not on an actual crime), blacks are an even bigger percentage of these convictions. Black Americans must recognize this, and understand that the ownership of firearms by blacks creates multiple problems: Created a requirement for 22,000 unconstitutional gun control laws. Undermined the spirit and intent of the Second Amendment. Assured that these gun control laws could not and would not work. Impaired the ability of all law-abiding citizens to defend themselves. Paralleled an almost tripling of the murder rate in the US. Enabled young American black men to achieve the world's highest sustained non-combat homicide rate. Contributed greatly to the murder of almost 0.2% of young black men each year. Put one million black men behind bars, more than are behind bars in all of Africa. Black people in general have sunk into a mire of behavior that leaves the average Joe/Jane scratching their heads profusely trying to   figure out these strange new mannerisms from a perspective of logic and reason. You see, when you remove logic and reason out of the equation, the way that most black people behave today appears to be normal. It is only when you inject logic and reason back into the mix are you then forced to be honest and truthful and call out the behavior for what it really is.

The focus of black people ideally should be to clean up that which is dirty within the community however instead most black people seem to think that the solution is to hide the dirt, refrain from addressing it and shoot down anybody who points out that there are some issues within the black nation that need to be dealt with. This is yet another example of the modern day black mindset of stupidity and foolishness and most black folks today are proud to be a part of an embrace this mindset with happiness and open arms. The first step towards restoration is actually admitting that there is a problem. Most black women and men have yet to even acknowledge this step forward. The black nation is trundling backwards rapidly and it is because of all of the above foolishness and more why we have not made any significant steps of progress within the last 70 years. Whether black folks like it or not, all of the above are signs of being effeminate. There is no reason for black boys and black men to be wearing pink in any garment, pink has always been and always will be a girl's color and no pink clothing promoting rappers are going to change this. This is the problem with this victim mentality, folks seem to think that they can do anything and that everything is ok. No everything is not ok and a man wearing pink as far as I am concerned indicates some serious underlying issues with that man. Why are you wearing skin tight jeans like a women black men? Since when was this deemed acceptable and who gave you that memo? This is simply yet again another classic sign of decadence among the black nation. Your trousers are supposed to be slack and of a loose fit. As ever, the so called Negro following and copying his European counterpart. I never thought in a million years that I would see this kind of clothing being sported by black folks in the US but it has happened for sure. Most black people by now have been informed as to where the sagging trousers phenomenon originated from yet many black folks especially the youth still embrace and exercise this act of stupidity, decadence and homo eroticism. Why black males who claim that they are not homosexual still hold the desire to show the whole world their underwear is beyond me. In cases like this you simply follow what black men do not what they say as following the words and not the actions will leave you as mentally confused as they are.

I hope you black men and boys who sag your trousers realize that when you walk down the streets in that fashion, the homosexual community have a field day looking at you rear end and wishing that they could dive in and indulge. If that is the type of attention that you want to draw to yourself then that is your business however, do not expect me to take the same route. My trousers will remain firmly around my waist where they are supposed to be positioned and where they belong. Many young Black men feel angry and are desperate because Black communities and America have failed them. While some of this hopelessness is understandable because of their extreme negative circumstances, it does not give any young Black man the right to hurt others. Let's begin with a controversial question: Are young Black men doing the work of the Ku Klux Klan as the primary killers of Black people in America? Without much debate, the answer is yes! Although the impetus for Black-on-Black destruction differs from the Klan's motivation, the results are arguably more horrific. Judging strictly by the numbers, the Klan was never as efficient as young Black men are today at killing Black people. According to a study from the Tuskegee Institute, the Ku Klux Klan killed 3,446 Black people in America during an 86-year span compared with Black men who kill about this same number of Black people every six months. Statistics from the United States Department of Justice clearly show the magnitude of this tragedy on U.S. soil, especially when compared with war-related data during a 9-1/2 year period from 2001 through 2010. In two U.S. wars, 6,754 American soldiers were killed (including 2,019 soldiers in Afghanistan since 2001 and 4,735 soldiers in Iraq since 2003). Statistics show that more than 7,000 Black people are murdered in this country every year! During the 9-1/2 years the U.S. has been at war overseas, about 67,000 Black people were murdered in the United States. Most of these homicides were committed by Black men, primarily men in the 17-44 year-old age range, against other Black men in that same age group. Black men comprise about 6.5 percent of the U.S. population and nearly half of U.S. homicide victims.

Today, the Black community faces a serious irony. Little more than 50 years ago, Black communities wanted Black men to protect them from White men who wore "hoods" while they killed Black people and destroyed their property. Fifty years later, Black communities are asking local (mostly White) police departments and state National Guard units to protect them from our sons and neighbors: mostly young Black men in "hoodies" and ski masks who are killing Black people and destroying their property. Whether perpetrated by the Ku Klux Klan or by young Black men, this terrorism is decimating Black communities. Opportunities for positive community development and growth are smothered when young Black men murder other young Black men and inadvertently maim and kill other innocent people in these communities. Children are afraid to travel to and from school, middle-income Blacks refuse to reside in high-crime communities, business owners steer clear of inner-city areas and senior citizens become easy prey. Black communities become paralyzed and implode under the weight of Black-on-Black crime, violence and murder. Five strategies, outlined by the U.S. Centers for Disease Control and Prevention, seem to offer the best approach to reduce youth violence and produce long-term, lasting, positive results. These recommended strategies include: (1) Build strong families and communities and employ responsible parents as the chief agents to reduce youth violence; (2) Teach young children ways to resolve conflict peacefully; (3) Provide mentors to serve as guides and role models for positive youth behavior; (4) Reduce social and economic causes of violence in young people's environments; and (5) Ensure spiritual or character-based training for young children and reinforce that training throughout their early teen years. Where is the official U.S. government's response to 67,000 Black American citizens slaughtered in its streets during the past 9-1/2 years? Implementing solutions that effectively   address this reign of death in the Black community will not and should not come primarily from Washington, state capitals or city halls. While it is the Black community that must strongly respond with effective solutions and actions, government still has a crucial responsibility to support structural remedies to this genocide. So far, local, state and federal governments alike have answered with a "calculated non-response" to the national carnage and human catastrophe of this Black-on-Black murder.

This same calculated non-response was the position taken by all levels of government during the reign of terror by the Ku Klux Klan. More than 145 years after the Klan's founding, only the killers have changed—not the killing, not the victims and not the poor response from government! Are young Black men doing the work of the Ku Klux Klan? They are doing it better than the Klan! And the world is watching. It is noted that although the reasoning for Black-on-Black killings may differ from the Klan's impetus, the results are in some black leaders words "arguably more horrific." The dates, parallel time lines, and related numbers sadly but factually speak for themselves. Noting a Tuskegee Institute study, a newsletter revealed that the Ku Klux Klan killed 3,446 Black people in America "during an 86-year span" as compared with Black men who kill about the same number of Black people "every six months."Backing up a Tuskegee documentation with this findings, authors Molefi K. Asante and Mark T. Mattson in their work "Historical and Cultural Atlas of African Americans" list that between the 29 years of 1889 and 1918 in the then 48 states from Alabama to Wyoming, 2,932 Black people were lynched. Comparatively, with our current 2010 Black-on-Black homicide stats, the authors chronicle the decade between 1890 and 1900 "as the most dangerous time" in the post Civil War era for Black men to be alive. They add that nearly 1,700 persons were lynched in that decade compared to 921 in the   decade between 1900 and 1910; 840 from 1910 to 1920, and nearly 400 between 1920 and 1930. Again, comparatively speaking, that would be 3,861 Black people killed by white hands between the 40 years of 1890 and 1930; still on the low end when measured against current day reported Black killings by Black hands. Statistics from the United States Department of Justice demonstrates the shockingly overwhelmed magnitude of this Black-on-Black reality during the nine-and-a-half year period from 2001 through 2010.

In two U.S. wars, 6,754 American soldiers were killed including 2,019 soldiers in Afghanistan since 2001 and 4,735 soldiers in Iraq since 2003. Shockingly for our nation's central city communities, the newsletter released data would reveal that during this same nine-and-a-half years that the U.S. has been at war oversees from 2001 through 2010, approximately 67,000 Black people were murdered during this same time in the United States. Yet another observer of stats comparing the killings of the Ku Klux Klan and the still growing Black-on-Black homicidal numbers is Clinton L. Black in his 2007 work "Why All Black People Are Coming to an End." According to his figures, the Ku Klux Klan lynched 3,437 Black men, women and children in the 115 years from 1866 to 1981. Today, he writes, Black people are murdering 3,437 Black men, women, and children in a 115 day period. Noting his findings, mathematically he postures that a Black person commits a crime against another Black person somewhere in America every second. His figures conclude that at this rate, that would be "six Black-on-black crimes a minute, 3,600 Black-on-Black crimes an hour, 86,400 Black-on-Black crimes a day, 604,800 Black-on-Black crimes a week, 2,629,743.83 Black-on-Black crimes a month, and 31,556,926 Black-on-Black crimes a year." The author contends that although the overwhelming majority of these crimes go unreported, this is still the most "devastating force" against Black people in the world today. Let's look at the numbers. For the purpose of this writing, we will use and anchor Black Star's figure of 67,000 Black-on-Black killings. Reviewing Black Star's Tuskegee figure of 3,447 Blacks killed by lynching, Black hands murdered 63,554 more Black folk then did whites during this present day period. Taking a look at Asante and Mattson's research of killings where 2,932 Blacks were lynched by whites. Black hands today murdered 64,068 more Black folk then did whites during the 29 years between 1889 and 1918. Since the U.S. has been at war oversees where approximately 6,754 American soldiers were killed, Black hands murdered 60,246 more Black folk then the numbers of reported Americans who died in Afghanistan and Iraq citing Black Star figures over the past nine-and-a-half- years from 2001 through 2010. And finally, we do not want to exclude author Clinton L. Black's findings.

According to his figures, the Ku Klux Klan murdered 3, 437 Black men, women and children. Black hands killed 63,563 more Black people within the past 10 years than did the Klan over the 115 years from 1866 to 1981. The majority of these crimes were committed by Black men primarily in the 17-44 year-old-age range against other Black men in that same age group. And although Black men may comprise only 6.5% of the U.S. population, such crime detailing accounts for nearly half of America's homicide victims. And here is a shameful present day irony. Exactly 118 years ago, Holly Springs, Mississippi born Ida B. Wells published a strong editorial in her paper "Free Speech" which brought her fame and nearly got her killed. A graduate of Rust College in Mississippi, Wells was a teacher, a journalist and Black America's most devoted crusader against lynching. But after her 1892 writing revealed names that were responsible for the lynching of three Memphis African Americans, a mob of whites demolished her printing press and office. They threatened to lynch Wells in front of the Memphis courthouse. But there was nothing new about such threats on her life. She had received her share of threats and hostilities from white men. She fled to New York City where she was hired by an African American weekly and launched her anti-lynching campaign. The Black Star newsletter contends that there was a time when Black communities "wanted Black men to protect them from white men who wore 'hoods' while these whites killed Black people and destroyed their property." Now today, Black communities in this age of "Our Black President" are no longer asking Black men to protect their/ or our families, women, children and property, but are pleading with (mostly white) police departments, state National Guard units and even the government to protect them/or us from our own Black males wearing "hoodies" and occasionally ski masks who are now in larger numbers killing Black people and destroying our property. "It's a Cultural Tragedy; no other people on earth hate, rape, rob, assault, envy, betray, distrust, kill, exterminate and outright violate Black people more than Black people! No other race of people in the whole world deliberately destroys their own people quite like Black people! In a real sense, we as a Black Community are a weapon of mass self-destruction!" says The Nation of Islam Leader Minister Louis Farrakhan. A 1982 study by sociologist Robert Staples titled, "Black Masculinity – The Black Male's Role in American Society," stated 28 years ago that:

"The largest group responsible for homicides in this country is that of Black males in the 20 to 24-year age range. And their victims are similarly young Black men – a fact which has as its most tragic consequence that homicide is listed as the number one cause of death among Black males aged 15 to 30." We have top the Black-on-Black homicide rates of 67,000 Black people between 2001 through 2010 or the stat reflecting that as of 2007/08, Black males in the U.S. having the lowest graduation rates ever amongst Black males as well as the College level. "Black students nationally score are at rock bottom on SAT and ACT with no outcry or action from leaders or parents." These scores "predict" low college admission rates, high unemployment rates and high incarceration rates. Black students are in trouble!" As well as the Black Community are in trouble and a positive and prideful Black future is in serious danger. What is more concern is why is it that for decade, we are continually witnessing the black community and particularly our children dying as a result of a slow but readily visible, understandable, and predictable self-imposed genocidal decay in our social, educational, political, and economic infrastructure while many of our so called black leaders, our ministers, our educators, our politicians, and our community stakeholders are saying and doing absolutely nothing. 145 years following 1865's Emancipation Proclamation, we can no longer use as an excuse or blame racism or White Supremacy for our Black community ills WE CANNOT!!!!!

Our President Barak Obama with the submission of any funds cannot all of a sudden raise us up with proposals for solutions at which point all with a 501 © 3 response as though your organization all of a sudden has some unique insight as to why our young men are killing one another or why our Black males are not graduating or why our students are scoring low on the ACT or SAT. It is us, our own people that have allowed this condition and self-destructive behavior to befall upon our youth as a result of our irresponsive inaction in this regard. Welcome to America where too many young Black men live short, desperate, miserable, complicated and violent lives. Recently a young Black man reported to the California General Assembly that the biggest challenge in his life was getting to school safely–not getting good grades or graduating from school, not wearing new clothes or even having a job, but just getting to school unscathed! Simply staying alive for 21 years is the number-one concern for many young Black men whose actions and inactions are influenced by their dire sense of hopelessness. Seemingly random negative obstacles facing Black males in America constitute nothing less than a well-crafted, highly orchestrated system of mass destruction for young Black men and boys. Black men and boys are at the bottom of the educational system and the top of the criminal justice system. Their life expectancy and health indicators are the lowest in America and they top the homicide and violent-injury statistics throughout the nation. Black males also rank at the bottom in high-school and college-graduation rates and at the top of the official and unofficial unemployment rates. All social indicators in America predict a short, miserable life for those unlucky enough to be born Black males in America. To what extent do Americans know and care enough to stop this systematic genocide? The New Jim Crow, a book written by Michelle Alexander, has become an instant classic and staple for college undergraduate and graduate classes in law, political science, sociology and history nationwide. It peels back the layers of modern, systematic racism that have led to more Black men in America being imprisoned in 2011 than there were Black people enslaved in America in 1850. A new "caste" system of racial control also has more Black men imprisoned in the United States today than the combined number of people imprisoned in every other country worldwide.

Yet there is optimism. Because of truth, passion, impatience, importance and power–like that found in such works as "Letter from a Birmingham Jail" and "Why We Can't Wait" by Dr. Martin Luther King, Jr. The New Jim Crow is away from policies, programs and practices that render America a horrifically unjust and hypocritical place. We must get to work making America great for all of us and let's invest in hope, cooperative action and opportunity for young Black men! "A young man was shot 41 times while reaching for his wallet"…"A 13-year-old was shot dead in mid-afternoon when police mistook his toy gun for a pistol"… "An unarmed young man, shot by police 50 times, died on the morning of his wedding day"… "A young woman, unconscious from having suffered a seizure, was shot 12 times by police standing around her locked car"… "The victim, arrested for disorderly conduct, was tortured and raped with a stick in the back of the station-house by the arresting officers." Does it surprise you to know that in each of the above cases the victim was Black? If you live in the USA, it almost certainly doesn't. Think what that means: that without even being told, you *knew* these victims. Those cases—and the thousands more like them that have occurred just in the past few decades—add rivers of tears to an ocean of pain. And they are symptoms of a larger, still deeper problem. But some today claim that America is a "post-racial society." They say the "barriers to Black advancement" have been largely overcome. Many go so far as to put the main blame for the severe problems faced by Black people today on…Black people themselves. Others claim that better education, or more traditional families, or religion, or elections will solve things. So the questions must be sharply posed: what really is the problem? What is the source of it? And what is the solution? We must know how the oppression of Black people has been at the very heart and functioning of this country, since its beginning and up to the present time, and what has actually *caused* these centuries of suffering. We must still analyze the massive struggles waged against this oppression, seeking still to understand why, even when they've won concessions; their powerful call for justice has been betrayed by the system each time.

While some disparities remain, things have generally advanced for Black people in America and today they are advancing still. Our President Barak Obama and Oprah are held up as proof. But have things really moved forward? Is this society actually becoming "post-racial"? The answer to that question can be found in every corner of U.S. society. Take employment: Black people remain at the bottom of the ladder, if they can find work at all. While many of the basic industries that once employed Black people have closed down, study shows employers to be more likely to hire *a white person with a criminal record* than a Black man without one, and 50% more likely to follow up on a resume with a "white-sounding" name than an identical resume with a "Black-sounding" name. The rate of unemployment for Black men is fully 48%. Or housing: Black people face the highest levels of racial residential segregation in the world—shunted into neglected neighborhoods lacking decent parks and grocery stores and often with no hospitals at all. Black people, as well as Latinos, who had achieved home-ownership had their roofs snatched from them. They were the ones hit hardest by the subprime mortgage crisis after having been targeted disproportionately by predatory lenders—resulting in the greatest loss of wealth to people of color in modern U.S. history. Or healthcare: Black infants face mortality rates comparable to those in the Third World country of Malaysia, and African-Americans generally are infected by HIV at rates that rival those in sub-Saharan Africa. Overall the disparities in healthcare are so great that one former U.S. Surgeon General recently wrote, "If we had eliminated disparities in health in the last century, there would have been 85,000 fewer black deaths overall in the early 2000's." Or education: Today the schools are more segregated than they have been since the 1960s with urban, predominantly Black and Latino schools receiving fewer resources and set up to fail. These schools more and more resemble prisons with metal detectors and kids getting stopped and frisked on their way to class by uniformed police who patrol their halls. Often these schools spend around half as much per pupil as those in the well-to-do suburbs. Or take imprisonment: The Black population in prison is 900,000, a tenfold increase since 1954! And the proportion of Black prisoners incarcerated relative to whites has more than doubled in that same period. A recent study pointed out that "a young Black male without a high school degree has a 59 percent chance of being imprisoned before his thirty-fifth birthday."

On top of all that, and reinforcing it, is an endlessly spouting sewer of racism in the media, culture and politics of this society—racism that takes deadly aim at the dreams and spirit of every African-American child. And who can forget the wave of nooses that sprung up around the country, south *and* north, in the wake of the 2007 struggle in Jena, Louisiana against the prosecution of six Black youth who had fought back against a noose being hung to intimidate them from sitting under a "whites only" tree at school? All this lay beneath the criminal government response to Hurricane Katrina in 2005. For reasons directly related to the oppression of Black people throughout the history of this country, and continuing today, African-Americans were..................... disproportionately the ones without the resources to get out of the way of that storm, as well as the ones concentrated in the neighborhoods whose levees had gone unrepaired for years. Far from "mere" incompetence, the government responded with a combination of gun-in-your-face............ repression and wanton, murderous neglect. People were stuck on rooftops in 100-degree heat for days on end, with nothing to eat or drink. Prisoners were left locked in cells as waters rose to their necks. The protection of private property and social control was placed above human life. The governor of the state ordered cops and soldiers to shoot on sight "looters"—that is, people trying to survive and to help others. On at least one occasion, people trying to escape the worst-hit areas were stopped by police at gunpoint from crossing over to a safer area. When evacuations finally *were* carried out, they were done with the heartlessness of a cruel plantation owner. Families were separated, with children ripped away from parents. Tens of thousands were scattered all over the country with one-way tickets, sometimes not even told their destinations. Back home, bodies were left floating in water, or lying on sidewalks, underneath debris, decomposing and mangled, for months. Through it all, politicians and commentators spewed out unrelenting racism. " A 10-term Congressman took the prize for declaring, "We finally cleaned up public housing in New Orleans. We couldn't do it, but God did."

Many parts of New Orleans still today are an uninhabitable ghost town. In the mostly Black 9th Ward, blocks of devastated houses have been razed—a vast wasteland now dotted with occasional concrete steps going nowhere. When Black people have fought to stay in the projects which are still habitable, they have been driven out—and when they have protested at City Council, they have been pepper-sprayed and beaten. Oil rigs and tourist areas are long since back up and humming, while rebuilding schools, hospitals, and childcare centers are pushed off the list. Through it all, cops continue to occupy poor neighborhoods like enemy territory. In opposition to the widespread notions of the............ "American dream," where each successive generation "does better" than the previous one, the majority of the children of middle-class Black families have been cast, by the workings of this system, onto a downward path. And many Black people—no matter how high they rise—still faces the insults and the dangers concentrated in the all-too-familiar experience of being stopped for "driving while Black." As Malcolm X said over 40 years ago, and as is still true today: What do they call somebody Black with a Ph.D.? A "nigger." And even more profoundly, for millions and millions of Black people, things have gotten WORSE. It will not help— in fact it will do real harm—to believe in this "post-racial" fantasy, or even the "less ambitious" lie of steady improvement. The cold truth of the oppression of African-American people must be squarely confronted and deeply understood, if it is ever to be transformed. This country was founded on the twin crimes of the genocidal dispossession of its Native American (Indian) inhabitants, and the kidnapping and enslavement of millions of Africans. But this essential and undeniable truth is constantly suppressed, blurred over, distorted and excused—all too often treated as "ancient history," if admitted at all. But let's look at its implications. Modern capitalism arose in Europe, when the merchant class in the cities—the newly arising capitalists, or *bourgeoisie*—began to set up workshops in which they exploited peasants who had been driven off their land, as well as others who could not make a living any longer other than by working for, and being exploited by, these capitalists. This was the embryo of the modern *proletariat*—a class of people who have no means to live except to work for someone else, and that works for wages in processes that require a collectivity of people working together.

The early capitalists, like their descendants, would take possession of and sell the goods thus produced, paying the proletarians only enough to live on, and thereby accumulating profit. They did this in competition with other capitalists, and those who could not sell cheaper were driven under; this generated a drive to gain any possible advantage, either through lowering wages and more thoroughly exploiting the working class, or through investing in more productive machinery, or both. This twin dynamic of exploitation and competition drove forward the accumulation of capital in a relentless and ever-widening cycle. But this was not some linear or self-contained process. In fact, capitalism in Europe "took off" with the development of the world market, and that in turn was fed and driven forward by the *slave trade*. Ships would sail from London and Liverpool, in England, filled with the goods sold by the capitalists. They would unload these goods for sale or trade in the coastal cities of Africa, and fill their holds with human beings who had been captured in raids in the African countryside. They would then take this human cargo to the Americas and the Caribbean, to be sold as slaves. Then the ships would take the sugar, cotton, rice and other goods produced by the slaves in these colonies back to Europe, to be sold for use as raw materials or food. And so on, every day, year in, year out—for centuries. This slave trade and the slave economy that went with it— along with the extermination of the Native peoples of the Americas (the Indians) through deliberate slaughter, disease, and working them to death in silver mines—formed what Karl Marx called the "rosy dawn of the primitive accumulation of capital." The crime was enormous. Between 9.4 and 12 million Africans were kidnapped, sold and sent to the Americas as slaves. Over two million more died in the voyage from Africa, and enormous numbers perished in Africa itself, through the slave-taking raids and wars, followed by forced marches in chains to the coastal African cities to feed this market. At least 800,000 more died in the port cities of Africa, locked down in prison (the barracoons) awaiting shipment. Once in the Americas, slaves were sent to "seasoning camps" to "break" them—where an estimated 1/3 of the Africans died in that first hellish year. Take a few seconds to think about the reality behind those numbers. THOSE WERE HUMAN BEINGS.

Those Africans who survived this hell were then forced to toil as slaves, doing the work to "tame" the Americas—to develop the agriculture that would form the basis for the new European colonies. A respected historian put it this way: "Much of the New World, then, came to resemble the death furnace of the ancient god Moloch—consuming African slaves so increasing numbers of Europeans (and later, white Americans) could consume sugar, coffee, rice, and tobacco." Within Africa itself, the slave trade caused tremendous distortions in the development of Africa and gave rise to the major African slave-trading states in West Africa, as these states traded slaves to the Europeans for commodities that included guns. Slavery existed in every part of the world and many societies before the transatlantic slave trade that began in the 1500s—but it had never before been carried out on this scale and with this nearly industrial-style inhumanity. That was the product not of uniquely evil men—but of men who *became* monsters by serving the demands of a monstrous new system whose only commandment was "Expand or Die." This slave trade was so integral to the rise of capitalism that the sugar and tea produced by slaves not only turned huge profits, but also served as a very cheap way to feed empty calories and stimulants to severely exploited proletarians in Europe. And the labor organization of the sugar cane fields of   Jamaica was adapted to the factory floors of London. To justify this, the capitalists and slave owners drew on the Bible—which yes, does in fact justify slavery, in both old testament and new testament—and then later on pseudo-scientific ideologies of racism that claimed that Africans and Native Americans (Indians) were a "lower species," inherently inferior. The fact that   Africans had been kidnapped, tortured, enslaved, killed if they tried to educate themselves, forced to watch as their children or spouses were sold off to other parts of the country, and generally kept in an inferior position—this CRIME by the *rulers* was pointed to as "proof" that Blacks were inferior. The fact that   Africans had been kidnapped, tortured, enslaved, killed if they tried to educate themselves, forced to watch as their children or spouses were sold off to other parts of the country, and generally kept in an inferior position—this CRIME by the *rulers* was pointed to as "proof" that Blacks were inferior.

Incredibly enough, these slaves were denounced as "lazy" by the parasitical slave masters whose great wealth the slaves created through their back-breaking labor! These lies served both to "justify" the horrors of slavery and formed a crucial element in the "social glue" that held society together. This pattern, and this lie and its social use, have continued in different forms up to today. The fact that these supposedly "inherently inferior" people had played a crucial part in building up highly developed societies and cultures in both Africa and the Americas, long before Europeans came to dominate these places, was an "inconvenient truth" written out of the official histories and textbooks. And the fact that all human beings are all one species, with only relatively superficial differences in some characteristics, was also written out, with spurious racist pseudo-science substituted instead—lies that also come up in new forms today. There was nothing inherent in Europeans that led to capitalism taking root there first—there were a number of areas in the world where capitalism might have taken off slightly earlier or slightly later if things had come together a little differently. But Europe is where capitalism did take off, and the dominance of the capitalist nations of Europe and then the U.S. (and Japan, which developed in a different set of circumstances) over the past five centuries is inconceivable without slavery. Slavery fueled the foundation and rise of not just capitalism in general, but the U.S. in particular. This is not just a "stain" that can   eventually be washed, or even scrubbed, away within the confines of this system; it is embedded in the very fabric of this society—indeed, the U.S. Constitution itself legally institutionalized slavery and deemed African-Americans to count as only 3/5 of a white person for census purposes. There is a semi-official narrative about the history and the "greatness" of America, which says that this greatness of America lies in the freedom and ingenuity of its people, and above all in a system that gives encouragement and reward to these qualities. Now, in opposition to this semi-official narrative about the greatness of America, the reality is that—to return to one fundamental aspect of all this—slavery has been an indispensable part of the foundation for the "freedom and prosperity" of the USA.

The combination of freedom and prosperity is, as we know, still today, and in some ways today more than ever, proclaimed as the unique quality and the special destiny and mission of the United States and its role in the world. And this stands in stark contradiction to the fact that without slavery, none of this—not even the bourgeois-democratic freedoms, let alone the prosperity—would have been possible, not only in the southern United States but in the North as well, in the country as a whole and in its development and emergence as a world economic and military power. Obviously, the way in which agriculture in the South developed was directly related to, indeed founded on, the system of slavery. But, beyond that, the way in which the U.S. related to the world market, and built up its prosperity and economic base in that way, was to a very large degree dependent on slave-based production. The interchange between the development of manufacture in the North and the development of agriculture in the South, for example—even when, before the Civil War, that interchange went to a large degree through the world market and through England in particular, where for example cotton would be sold to the textile mills in England and other products would be sold from England to the northern manufacturers in the U.S. —even that would not have happened in the way it did, on the kind of scale it did and with the prosperity that it led to, without slavery. Of course, this process—where, for example, cotton from the southern U.S. was to a large degree sold to England, rather than to New England—contributed over time to sharpening the contradiction between the slave system in the South and the developing capitalist system in the North of the U.S. But the point to emphasize here is that, in an overall and fundamental sense, the slave-grown products of the southern U.S. constituted a major factor in the development of the U.S. economy, in the North as well as the South. And the development of that economy, in turn, has been the essential underlying basis for the massive military machinery which is the ultimate enforcer of the role of the U.S. as a major world power. This poisonous master-class mentality did not die with the abolition of slavery—it continued, in new forms. In particular, each wave of immigrants that came over from Europe had to "fit itself into" the dominant relations of American society—they had to find an "economic niche" (usually toward the bottom rungs of the working class, at least at first) and they had to work out a relation to the dominant political and cultural superstructure of society.

In doing so, these white immigrants often tried to distinguish themselves from Black people—and this often exploded into the open antagonism of white mobs rampaging against Black people and even lynching them—yes, in the northern cities as well as the South, as these immigrant communities defined themselves as "full-blooded" white Americans *in violent opposition* to Black people. This system reinforced the master-class mentality among northern whites with petty, but not insignificant, privileges in jobs and housing. And this became a major double-barreled shotgun for the capitalist ruling class: it blinded these white people and immigrants to their most fundamental interests as members of the proletariat, turning their anger away from the system that actually exploited and oppressed them, and turning it against the most oppressed and exploited people in society. And it gave them an "identity" as *white* Americans, with a set of expectations and entitlements to go with it—and to defend. A minority of whites opposed this madness, and took up revolutionary or radical or even just decently humane positions; but while very important—and we'll return to its significance later—this sort of stand was far too uncommon. (A secondary, but important, effect of this master-class mentality among whites of all classes was to partly obscure the *class* character of the oppression of the masses of Black people—their position and role as viciously exploited *proletarians*, within the overall working class of the U.S.—and the many and close links between this *class exploitation* of large numbers of Black people, as part of the proletariat, and the *national oppression* of Black people as a people.) To return again to the period of slavery, it is important to be clear on an essential truth: the slaves fiercely resisted this. In the U.S. alone there were over 200 slave revolts, and the slaves of Haiti stunned the world when they successfully waged a 15-year revolution against first their colonial masters, then the British, and finally Napoleon's armies. Even with these heroic revolts, it was only with the Civil War that the resistance finally bore fruit in the U.S., and the emancipation of Black people from outright slavery was achieved. Here too the masses of Black people—both runaway slaves and "freedmen"—played a crucial role. When finally allowed to join the Union Army, they died at twice the rate of white soldiers (while being paid lower wages for most of the Civil War)! The Civil War itself came about because of the clash between two different economic and social systems: slavery, based on plantation farming in the South; and capitalism, based on factory and other wage-labor centered in the North.

The slave owners needed more land because their plantation system of farming used up the land so fast, while the northern capitalists wanted to control the country as a whole, both for resources and to further develop their control of the national market. By the time of the Civil War, these two forces—these two social systems—were clashing on virtually every major question of economics. For example, factory production was just getting going in the North, and these northern capitalists wanted to erect high tariffs (in effect, taxes on imported goods) to secure the U.S. National market and "protect" their industries against the English capitalists, who could produce things much more cheaply; but the slave-holders   insisted on low tariffs to enable them to easily trade with those same English manufacturers. And these basic economic conflicts found expression in politics, culture, and even religion—the Baptist and Methodist churches, among others, split into northern and southern branches over the "godliness" (or "ungodliness") of slavery! Why? Simply because people in the North had become enlightened? No. While there *was* a surge of more radical thinking in the North in the decades prior to the Civil War, and militant opponents of slavery such as Frederick Douglass and John Brown began to get a hearing and gain a following, this was ultimately an expression of more fundamental changes going on in the economic base of society—that is, the relations that people enter into to carry out production—and the intensifying contradictions within that economic base, and between that economic base and the political structure which had arisen on top of it. In short, slavery had changed from being the stimulus that it was in the early days of capitalism into a fetter on the development of capitalism. The constitution that served the economic base of 1789—a constitution which legalized and institutionalized slavery—could no longer contain the intensified contradictions of 1860. Abraham Lincoln himself, the president of the United States during the time of the Civil War, was the political representative of the bourgeoisie—the factory-owners, railroad-owners, and other capitalists centered in the North—and he fought the war in their interests. In the view of Lincoln, the power of the slave states had to be at minimum sharply curtailed; and it was only when he was convinced that there was no other way forward that he went to war.

Similarly, Lincoln delayed emancipating the slaves and then delayed allowing the slaves to enlist in the Union army until he was convinced that there was no other way to carry out his basic aim of "saving the Union." Lincoln himself said: My paramount object in this struggle *is* to save the Union, and is *not* either to save or destroy Slavery. If I could save the Union without freeing *any* slave, I would do it; and if I could save it by freeing *all* the slaves, I would do it; and if I could do it by freeing some and leaving others alone, I would also do that. The aftermath of the Civil War presented the now predominant capitalist class with an opportunity to truly integrate the freed slaves into the larger society. The slaves had poured generations of labor into the foundation of the society and then died way out of proportion to their numbers in the Civil War. Northern generals during the war had promised the freed slaves "40 acres and a mule." As a matter of simple, basic justice it would have been right to divide the land that they had worked for generations among the former slaves, as well as the non-slaveholding whites; and as a matter of having a basis for political freedom, doing this was imperative. And it was imperative as well that these former slaves have the full political rights they had fought and died for—including the right to suppress the bitter, unrepentant ex-Confederate soldiers who, already in the waning days of the Civil War, were forming into secret paramilitary societies to violently attack the freed slaves and "preserve the southern way of life." But this was not done. Indeed, the true interests of the northern capitalists came out with their betrayal of Reconstruction. During this all too brief period of Reconstruction, in the 10 years or so after the end of the Civil War, the U.S. government had kept some of its promises and stationed troops in the South. These troops were there to prevent wholesale slaughters of Black people, and poor whites, who were striving to gain land and exercise political rights promised to them. But the capitalist class which now dominated the national government did this in large part in order to fully subordinate the former plantation owners; and when the ex-slaves and their allies fought "too hard" for their rights these same troops would be used against them. Above all the northern capitalists wanted order and stability to carry out the further consolidation of their rule, as well as further expansion on the North American continent and internationally.

The ferment and upheaval that would have gone along with everything that would have been involved in the former slaves playing a significant role in the political process or even exercising basic rights might have "sent the wrong message" to other oppressed people within the U.S.; and in fact, when in 1877 the U.S. troops were pulled out of the South, signaling the end of Reconstruction, they were immediately sent west—to fully crush the resistance of the Indians—and into the cities of the North—to violently suppress revolts of immigrant workers. Further, real freedom for the former slaves would have enabled them to resist the severe exploitation that was visited upon them, and thus would have made the re-integration of the southern economy into the larger society much less profitable for the ruling capitalists. So the Ku Klux Klan was unleashed in full force and played a brutal role in defeating and subjugating the freed slaves and progressive whites, often in bloody battles. Then the Supreme Court "made it all legal," with the *Cruikshank* decision—which upheld the state of Louisiana's decision to not prosecute the white perpetrators of the massacre of over 100 Black and white supporters of Reconstruction in Colfax, Louisiana—and *Plessy v. Ferguson*, which enabled states to legally segregate Black people. In short, when the opportunity for integration on an equal footing into this society arose in the period after the Civil War, the "demands" of the economic base of the capitalist system, and the political superstructure that arises on and serves that base, overrode that opportunity…and the answer was NO. Equality was denied—and this denial was enforced through the most bloodthirsty means. The new social order that came with the betrayal of Reconstruction forced most Black people into the position of working the land for white plantation owners in relations that were barely better than slavery. And some forms of the actual, literal enslavement of Black people continued, particularly in the South, long after slavery had been legally abolished. The masses of Black people were kept chained to the land by debt, by legal discrimination…and by violence. Through all this, rather than being integrated on an equal basis into U.S. life, Black people were forged into an oppressed nation within the Black Belt South during this period—denied all democratic rights, including the right to self-determination as a nation. Shortly after the Civil War, the capitalist system made a leap to a new stage—to a worldwide system of imperialism, which divided up the entire globe among a handful of powers. The re-entrenchment of white supremacy in a new form, after the Civil War, formed an important element in the U.S.'s rise to major power status among these imperialists.

The cotton and tobacco produced by the bitterly exploited Black sharecroppers were the top cash crops of the U.S. from 1850 to 1890, and Black men who were arrested by southern sheriffs on the flimsiest of charges and literally sold as slave labor built the industrial infrastructure of the South. (early, documentation was noted of the use of over 100,000 Black people in slave labor industrial projects, and the actual number is undoubtedly far higher than the 100,000 has been documented. Conditions in these camps, including widespread disease, systematic degradation, torture, including "water boarding," and a high death rate, call to mind the concentration camps of Nazi Germany.) At the same time, the reinforcement of the master-class mentality among large sections of whites strengthened their identification with the ruling class. And the reintegration of the southern ruling class elements into the larger capitalist class—with the southerners getting particular power in the Congress and being a major force in the military—reinforced the ruling class as a whole in its cohesiveness. The white American tradition of lynching—where mobs of people drag someone out of their homes, or even out of jail, and hang them for some real or, more often, imagined crime without benefit of a trial—played a very important role in all this. Nearly 5,000 people were lynched between 1882 and 1964, with over 70% of them Black. Sometimes these lynching's were carried out under cover of darkness—but often these were "community affairs," attended by thousands of whites, in a carnival atmosphere, who would then have pictures taken of themselves posing with the often burnt and mutilated body of the victim, sometimes making these photographs into postcards to send to friends. The *Cruikshank* decision, mentioned earlier, gave a legal green light to this kind of barbaric terror; and for decades the U.S. Senate refused to pass laws calling for federal action against lynching. In short, the ruling class backed these lynching's to the hilt. Usually, the victims were poorer Blacks—but often the one committing the lynching went after the small minority of Blacks who owned land. In 1916, Anthony Crawford of Abbeville, S.C., a Black cotton farmer who owned 427 acres of prime land and had started a Black school in the area and a union for Black people, was lynched after a dispute with a white man over the price of Crawford's cotton crop.

He was hanged from a pine tree and shot over 200 times, and whites drove his family from the area and divided up his land. In fact, a few years ago the Associated Press documented over 57 violent land-takings by whites. But the hellish social function served by lynching's was larger than sheer greed, larger than reinforcing racist feelings (and intimidating any who might resist) through grisly barbaric rituals. It was to enforce a social system in which Blacks were to be chained to the land through terror—, one part of that was to crush any Blacks who might form the makings of a "national bourgeoisie" among Black people which might not be as pliant as the Booker T. Washington's of the era and which might, therefore, upset the established order of things by demanding the rights associated with being a nation. (Booker T. Washington was the founder and head of the Black college Tuskegee Institute, and preached that while there were "problems" in the South, Blacks should advance by learning trades and working hard, while submitting to oppression, and in THAT way they could improve their position within the system in this country; he was promoted by the ruling class as the spokesman for Black people and became the prototype of the "responsible Negro leader," and echoes of his line can be heard today in Bill Cosby—and Barack Obama.) It is a bitter irony that many of the whites who today cling to the "grand narrative" —that people in America, or rather *white* people, have made it due to their ingenuity and hard work, taking advantage of the "freedom" offered by this society—and who complain about things like affirmative action—conveniently forget that at the very time that most Black people were being forced onto the land as sharecroppers (essentially a form of semi-slavery), with those who did own property often having it violently ripped from them, including through murder…at that very time, the ancestors of these whites were being given land that had been forcibly stolen from the Native Americans, and these whites were sending their children to "land grant" colleges set up by the government to teach them advanced farming techniques, or else getting help from "agricultural agents" also sent out by the government. This opportunity to get a farm, and to get government support in getting that farm up and running, not only served as a "steam valve" for the discontent of many exploited white people, it also further fed into the master-class mind-set and assumptions prevalent among white people about "what it means to be an American."

It was only with World War 2—nearly 100 years after the Civil War—that a major change began to be brought about in the situation of Black people in the U.S. Around the time of World War 1, there was a big demand for workers in the defense plants and other factories, at the same time as the war cut off the flow of immigrant labor from Europe. Capital needed workers—and so some Black people were drawn from the South and allowed in—on the bottom floor. This flow was delayed by the economic depression of the 1930s, but with the outbreak of World War 2 there was once again a huge demand for labor. Then, on top of that, the years directly after World War 2 brought the mechanization of agriculture in the South—so now Black people were not only being drawn to the northern factories, they were being *driven off* the land that they had farmed for generations under conditions of extreme exploitation. The forms of oppression differed in the North, but the fact of oppression remained the same. African-American workers were brought into the workforce, but on the basis of their oppression as a people they were put into the dirtiest, most dangerous and lowest-paying jobs. They were "last hired and first fired." Black people were refused the subsidies that white people received to buy houses, and even when Blacks had the money they were prevented, either by unspoken agreements, government policy, or straight-up violence by white mobs and/or vigilantes (usually assisted by the police), from buying homes in "white" neighborhoods. Instead they were shunted—by government policy—into poorly built high rise housing projects in the inner cities. African-Americans faced segregation and discrimination everywhere they turned, North and South. But the changes in the South, in the context of major political changes internationally, had given rise to a civil rights movement. Black people were marching, demanding very basic and fundamental rights—the right to vote, to equal education, to not be humiliated when they tried to use public facilities. They were met with police dogs, bombs and Ku Klux Klan terror. Indeed, over 25 civil rights workers were murdered in the South. This time, however, a different dynamic came into play: once things reached a certain point, the more that the power structure came at them, the more the masses fought back. And this interacted with the international challenges facing the U.S. ruling class at the time. The oppressed nations and colonies were rising up and fighting for national liberation in the "Third World" of Asia, Africa and Latin America.

Revolutionary China, under the leadership of Mao Tsetung, was exerting a galvanic pole of attraction within that situation, powerfully reviving the goal and ideology of communism and inspiring people all over the world to seek out the ways to make revolution—against an imperialist order headed by the U.S. The U.S. rulers were also contending with the formerly socialist Soviet Union (which had become imperialist but had not yet dropped its socialist cover) and old-line colonial powers, particularly Britain and France, for influence in the Third World. In the face of all this, the struggle against the continuing barbarity of the oppression of the Black people in the South—and the way that struggle kept forcing this question onto the world's front pages—was compelling the American ruling class to scramble, and to make adjustments in how it dealt with Black people. So all this—the indomitable growth of the southern-based civil rights movement in the 1950s and early '60s and the ways in which it was becoming not just a nationwide but a worldwide "force of attraction," along with the migrations to the "promised land" of the North, raised expectations. But the reality of this system once again dashed these heightened hopes. African-Americans in the North continued to be subject to blatant oppression and discrimination. And the southern lynch mobs found their cowardly counterpart in northern mobs that would burn out Black people who would dare to buy houses in "white neighborhoods," or would attack Black children who dared to go to "white schools." The masses answered this question, unmistakably. People rebelled in hundreds of American cities, and the revolutionary stance of leaders like Malcolm X and forces like the Black Panther Party resonated with millions in the streets and campuses of the U.S. Many things fed into this—including, again, the international situation which, as pointed out earlier, was marked by a great upsurge in national liberation struggles and the influence of a socialist China under the leadership of Mao. With this powerful upsurge hammering the walls of the social order, some barriers to Black people did fall. Some African-Americans were given opportunities to enter college and professional careers, and social programs like welfare, community clinics, and early education programs were expanded. Government spending for training and jobs that would employ Black people increased. Some discrimination was lifted in credit for housing and small businesses.

Most of this was in the form of small concessions—not only did this not begin to touch the real scars of hundreds of years of terrible oppression, but discrimination *continued* in all of these arenas. Nonetheless, these advances were hardly insignificant. Even more important than these particular concessions, in some ways, were the "intangibles."The consciousness of not just African-Americans but other minorities, and many millions of white people as well, radically changed. People sharply challenged the lies that for decades had been taught in American schools and had been driven home in American culture through works like *Gone With the Wind* and *Birth of a Nation*. The REAL history of slavery, the Civil War, Reconstruction, and the whole period of the 20th century began to be unearthed and brought forward. The '60s showed that a movement that had Black people as its most solid base of support and the struggle for their emancipation as its leading edge, and that drew connections to other outrages of the system and other struggles against that system, could also inspire and draw forward people of other oppressed nationalities within the U.S., students of all nationalities, and then spread as well to women, to white proletarians ("poor whites"), soldiers and beyond. All kinds of people began to look at everything about this society with fresh eyes—and with the blinders suddenly taken off, they didn't like what they saw and decided to question it and fight it! To put it another way, the '60s showed that when masses rose up in rebellion against the powers-that-be, and when that was coupled with a political stance that called out the system as the problem, and when a growing section of that movement linked itself to and learned from the revolutionary movement worldwide...well, when all that happened, you could radically change the political polarization in society. What could hardly be imagined yesterday suddenly became a real possibility for tomorrow, which demanded action today. (Some of these same phenomena, in microcosm, also occurred in the Los Angeles Rebellion of 1992, over the acquittal of the police who had beaten Rodney King. While the initial spark came from the Black masses, significant numbers of Latinos and whites, especially the youth, either joined in or politically supported it, and many, many people were at least temporarily drawn into political life and some to a much more radical and even revolutionary political outlook.)

The '60s also dramatically showed that the rulers of this system, for all their power and viciousness, are not *all*-powerful—not when the people whom they rule over rise up and rebel in their hundreds of thousands and then millions. Seriously challenged and battered by the Vietnam War and the struggle "at home," these rulers actually fell into serious disarray, and sharp battles broke out within their ranks, which provided further "oxygen" for upsurge from below. In many respects, the ruling class was put on the political defensive, and even lost its "legitimacy" in the eyes of millions. This whole upsurge within the U.S. also had a tremendous effect internationally—both exposing America's lying pretensions about its "free society" and giving inspiration to the masses in countries all over the world. But while this tremendous struggle brought down some barriers to formal equality, and while the rulers were challenged and the system shaken to its foundations, the people were not able to make revolution. And here we have to make an important point: revolution is not just a cool word that means "lots of change"; revolution has a very specific meaning. It means that the people *overthrow* the system and deprive its rulers of their political power and, as the essence of that power, the ability to wield armies and police against the people. Revolution further means that a new power is then established, with new aims and objectives and the means to enforce those aims and objectives. There WAS a revolutionary *movement* in the '60s—and that is something of monumental significance. But there was NOT a revolution—and that too has monumental significance, in understanding what did happen...what didn't happen...and what must yet happen. The elimination of some formal discrimination, the expansion of a middle stratum of Black people, and the emergence of a few "Black faces in high places" did not and could not tear up the deep roots of white supremacy (nor still less bring about the broader emancipation that was needed). And the elimination of formal discrimination also could not deal with the class position of the masses of Black people—as members of the proletariat, the property less class that is either directly exploited by capitalists or kept as part of the desperately impoverished "reserve army of the unemployed" which can be more readily and ruthlessly exploited when it serves the capitalists' purposes, and which the capitalists seek to use to depress the conditions and fighting spirit of the proletariat overall.

The struggle of the African-American people for liberation is tied by a thousand threads to the struggle of the proletariat for the full emancipation of all humanity. There is no brick wall between these forms of oppression—they are constantly intertwining and interpenetrating, as was seen in Hurricane Katrina. Indeed, there is a common enemy at the root of both these forms of oppression—the capitalist-imperialist system. There is a common solution to both—communist revolution—and the proletariat, as a class, has no interest in maintaining any form of oppression and every interest in wiping out all forms of oppression. Because there was no revolution in the U.S. in the 1960s and, along with that, because the revolutionary struggle internationally ultimately suffered serious setbacks, the decades since has been a nightmare. The power of the ruling class had been shaken, but not overthrown; and they came back with a vengeance. Major transformations went on in the international political and economic structure of imperialism during these past decades. Here we can only indicate, in basic terms, some of the main aspects of all this, which includes:

• the strategic rivalry, up through the 1980s, between the U.S. and the Soviet Union (which contained the real danger of nuclear war);

• the subsequent fall of the Soviet Union in the early 1990s, and the heightening globalization of capital that followed in its wake. Among other things, this accelerated the uprooting of hundreds of millions of peasants, who were driven into the cities of the Third World, as well as the imperialist countries, as sources of low-wage labor;

• the U.S.'s strategic decision to launch the "war on terror"—which is in fact a war to construct an unchallenged and unchallengeable empire, and which also draws on and unleashes the most backward and reactionary forces in this society as its base of support.

All these developments have been decisive in setting the context in which the ruling class of this country has moved to deal with the still unresolved role of Black people within U.S. society, in the aftermath of the great upsurge of the 1960s, which, as we have spoken to here, shook this system and its ruling class to their foundations but which was not able to bring about a fundamental change through an actual revolution.

As the '60s ended, concessions had barely been given before, in every sphere, they began to be snatched away. The ruling class brought in Nixon as president, and he pursued dual tactics. On the one hand, he declared himself in favor of "Black power" and built up some Black businesses in an effort to pacify a section of the middle class. But his overwhelmingly principal edge was repression. The sharpest blade of this was brought down against the Black Panther Party: hundreds of its members—including key leaders—were framed up and imprisoned, and over 20 of its members—again, including key leaders like Fred Hampton and George Jackson—were assassinated. The Nixon regime also brutally repressed other rebellious sections of society—as seen in the murders of antiwar students at Kent State and the all-Black Jackson State in Mississippi. Nixon also developed the "southern strategy" of the Republican Party, which nakedly appealed to the racism of unrepentant reactionary southern whites and gave these, and other reactionary forces, political legitimacy and initiative. Meanwhile, the Democratic Party made moves to bring a whole section of Black activists from the '60s into the arena of bourgeois electoral politics. Both parties worked to develop "frontiers"—"Black faces in high places" who purported to act as brokers between the masses and the powers, but in actual fact weighed down the people's ability to resist through lack of leadership and lies. The upheaval of the '60s had once again powerfully presented a clear challenge to the ruling class to eliminate white supremacy and integrate Black people into society on an equal footing. Once again, this was **NOT** done. The promise of equality was once more betrayed—as it had been after the Civil War. And once again, two things were at work: the needs of capital, which continued to gain advantage from racist discrimination and ghetto life of millions of African-Americans; and the necessity of the capitalists to not disrupt—and in fact to reassert and reinforce with a vengeance—the social glue of white supremacy—the ways in which the lie of the "master class" were so integral to so many people's understanding of "being American." This was important for the ruling class, particularly going into a volatile period when the U.S. was both coming off defeat in Vietnam and facing potentially far greater challenges abroad. Meanwhile, major changes were developing in the ways in which Black people were "inserted into" the economic relations of society.

The search for the highest possible profit, along with the increasing ability to invest capital all over the globe, resulted in the disappearance of many industrial jobs in the inner cities of the U.S. Some were shifted to the suburbs—where capitalists moved their facilities, in part to keep African-Americans out of their work force, since they considered them too rebellious—and some overseas. Between 1967 and 1987, the four cities of Philadelphia, Chicago, New York and Detroit together lost over *one million* factory jobs—and this trend has only accelerated in the decades since! At the same time, the radical transformations and plundering of the economies of the Third World drove new workers to the U.S. (and other imperialist countries)—with today an estimated 12 million of these workers in the U.S. lacking any legal papers, and hence living at the mercy of the capitalist ruling class. Black people had, ever since the 1950s made up a disproportionate section of the reserve army of the   unemployed, in and out of work, often having to hustle to get by; today this has expanded and intensified to a whole other level. In 1969, H.R. Haldeman, Nixon's top assistant, wrote in his diary that "[President Nixon] emphasized that you have to face the fact that the whole problem is really the blacks. The key is to devise a system that recognizes this while not appearing to." Thus was born the "war on drugs." Launched by Nixon, this "war on drugs" was taken to a whole other level by Reagan, who became president in 1980. It marked a strategic decision by the ruling class to maintain inner-city Black youth in desolate hyper-segregated neighborhoods which lacked jobs, and where education and health care resources had been severely cut. Even with the jobs that remained, discrimination was stepped up, as employers sought to avoid the "defiance" of Black youth who, were "not so pliant for capitalist exploitation." Instead of providing better education and the promise of new opportunities for these youth, drugs would be allowed to flood the inner city, and many inner-city youth would be funneled into the drug trade—where they would then be vulnerable to constant harassment, arrest, imprisonment and social isolation. The rate of imprisonment exploded drastically to the point where shuttling between the hard hustle of the streets and the harder times in prison became the dominant mode of life in many oppressed inner-city communities—a lifetime of lockdowns. Beginning at that time and continuing and intensifying up through today, whenever jobs open up in a major city, people will line up for blocks to even get a chance to apply.

But for most of the time—and, in some areas, for most of the people—there is little choice other than the illegal economy. On that basis, the "code of the streets" took significantly deeper root: that is, the rules of survival borne of the shark-like competition of the illegal economy set terms for inner-city youth more broadly, with the resulting horrific "Black-on-Black" violence and violence between Black and Latino youth that the mainstream, bourgeois commentators deplore, or pretend to deplore. And the conservatives launched an incredible campaign of demonization of Black youth in particular, right down to inventing a category of "feral super-predators" to justify the massive wave of criminalization. During this same period, the cons launched a truly vicious campaign of demonization and humiliation against Black women on welfare. No insult was out of bounds for these racist conservatives. Going along with all this—and very consciously built up as part of this reactionary counter-offensive by the ruling class—has been the revival of the Black church and religious feeling among Black people. The influence of religion had in fact greatly ebbed during the latter part of the '60s, when people raised their heads to fight for revolution and, as part of doing so, struggled to rationally figure out how the world really worked and how to change it. But with the ebb of the revolutionary struggle at the end of that decade, feelings of disorientation and despair arose among many. Religious forces raced to fill that void with all kinds of erroneous, objectively harmful, and in some cases outright reactionary and deadly ideas: blaming yourself for being oppressed by this system; seeing capitalism as the way out of a madness that was caused by capitalism; strengthening male domination over women; substituting Bible stories and mythology for the actual truths of science (including evolution) and generally pushing the idea that people can't really understand the world, and therefore can't really go about changing it radically, and so must "leave it to the lord." Whether these ideas were being run by many pastor, preacher/teacher (whose militant posing conceals a profoundly conservative—and in many ways outright reactionary—brand of nationalism), they all confused, misled and demoralized people.

Today, *as they did in slavery times,* the capitalist ruling class builds up the church as the MAIN institution in the Black community. Government money that once went to public education and community arts is now channeled through preachers who align themselves with the government and with the Christian fascist movement that has been built up by Bush. Nowhere is this sharper than in the prisons. The struggle of the '60s spurred among prisoners a thirst for knowledge and truth, and they fought for and won the right to take college courses and have access to literature even though they were locked up; today that is increasingly suppressed and flushed away while reactionary fundamentalist "prison ministries" are given total access to the minds of the literally millions of Black youth whom the system shuttles through these hellholes, with large numbers at any given time serving long sentences in degrading prison conditions. While many religious people and clergy oppose, and can be united in struggle against, the outrages and crimes of this system, and important aspects of the oppression of Black people and others, there must be struggle and debate over the real character of the problem and solution, and the worldview and method that is necessary to win complete emancipation, and the real role of religion in relation to all that. Religion—both in general and particularly in the more recent period— plays the role of turning people away from seeking a real understanding of the actual causes and dynamics of things, as they really are, and the possibility of changing things in this real world. Even when more "progressive" versions of religion may encourage people to resist oppression (or particular aspects of oppression), it still promotes the idea that, when all is said and done, people themselves cannot change things by consciously seeking out and coming to an understanding of what is the problem—what is the actual cause of people's situation and where oppression actually comes from—and waging a determined struggle on the basis of that understanding, but instead they must ultimately put things "in the hands of a god" and rely on this non-existent god to give them the courage and strength to persevere. And things are worse, on a whole other level, with the reactionary religious viewpoints that openly uphold this system and the key pillars of its oppressive relations.

The hope and optimism of the '60s, founded on the real potential that can be seen when people rise up, fight back and begin to seek out a radical alternative to this monstrous system...this hope has turned to despair in the face of decades of betrayal and brutal repression meted out by these rulers, decades of needless suffering and unforgivable squandering of human potential. Today the situation is even more dangerous. To take one stark example: there is the distinct possibility, and there are already definite trends and developments toward, a whole new era of "neo-slavery," where a predominantly Black prison population is put to work for pennies a day, either to turn profits for capitalists or bring down costs for the state. And there are those in the ruling class making "policy suggestions" with genocidal implications— people like the prominent Republican and fundamentalist Christians who has advocated executing not only people convicted of murder, but any people who commit crimes that "put a stain" on society. For one thing, while many things are the same—including the oppression of Black people as a central fact of American life and how that would be reflected—many things, including some of the particular forms in which Black people are oppressed, have changed significantly in the four decades since the '60s. For another thing, the movement of that time had real limitations. Even the most radical forces in that movement— including Malcolm X and the Black Panther Party—were not clear on what the aims of a revolution should be, and on how really deeply seated in the *capitalist* system are the oppression of Black people and the other forms of oppression that people were rising up against. For Malcolm, and to a large extent even the Panthers, the horizons of the struggle did not go beyond the liberation of Black people as a people, there was not a completely clear and correct understanding of how that liberation could actually be achieved, and there was at least a trend of "forcing America to keep its promises." But there is a reason that America has continually betrayed "its promises": the oppression of the African-American people forms an *essential* part of the fabric and functioning of U.S. society, and any attempt to uproot it would tear up the whole fabric of this society as it now exists.

Further, the emancipation of the African-American people—who not only make up an oppressed nation *within* the larger society but also are, in very large numbers, members of the U.S. social class—is bound up with the revolution led by the social class for the full emancipation of all humanity. There was confusion when some of the formal legal barriers to advancement were removed, and a small section of the oppressed were able to move up, even if in limited ways, while the majority of the masses were ground into even worse conditions. The notions that were brought forward to explain this—that many movements failed or, worse yet, that the people failed to take advantage of "their new opportunities"—are wrong and extremely damaging. Some say the movement did not fail; *it did not go far enough.* And that not only were the "doors to opportunity" never really or fully opened, even more fundamentally there were still thousands of steel threads, some visible and some hidden, that were deeply embedded in society and holding the *masses* of Black people down. Something more radical, more thorough going, was and is needed. Let's take the glaring contradiction of the inner-city streets where the crying need for decent housing, schools, health care, and cultural and recreation facilities exists side-by-side with young people who haunt those same street corners, and can find no other employment but the drug trade. Under capitalism nothing can be done unless it serves the further accumulation of capital and the political interests of the capitalist ruling class, and this requirement stands as a barrier between the work that society needs and the masses that could do it. So either these neighborhoods are left to rot, or they are transformed by capital into "high-end" housing which is more profitable—and which ends up driving the basic social masses out. Take another literally killing contradiction of this current system: the sharp conflict between Black and Latino masses. The driving compulsions of capitalist accumulation uprooted Africans and brought them in chains to America as slaves, and then put them through 400 years of hell. The same relations of capital drove the conquistadors from Europe to Mexico and South America to colonize and subjugate the   native inhabitants (the ones that they did not wipe out altogether); and those same compulsions resulted in the later subjugation by the United States of Mexico and other parts of Latin America, the plunder of those countries, and the eventual driving of millions of people from those countries *into* the U.S., desperately seeking any work they could get.

The spontaneous workings of these same relations have pitted these peoples against each other. Immigrants are put to work in terrible jobs and at the same time subjected to repression just for living—and as this is done, they are told that Black people are too lazy to take those jobs and should be scorned, and are further told that if they work hard and keep their heads down and suck up to this country's rulers, proving that they believe in the "American dream," they will get ahead. Meanwhile, Black people in many parts of the country are largely thrown to the side by this same social class that pumped out their labor for so many years, generation after generation, and are told that "the Mexicans are taking your jobs," and that Black people should quit being so defiant and instead stand up for their status as "true Americans." All the while the education system and media reinforce these divisions—on the one hand, hiding from the different peoples how they have, in many ways, shared a similar fate, brought about by oppression at the hands of a common enemy; and on the other, constantly framing things in such a way so as to aggravate the divisions caused by the world system, and how it sets people against each other, including through competition for jobs and resources. While important strides can and must be made in changing this, in developing unity among exploited and oppressed people of all different nationalities in building a **Kingdom Community**, these divisions cannot be fully overcome without finally getting rid of capitalism and bringing a radically different world into being. But let's imagine a Kingdom Community in which the economic system provides jobs for *everyone* able to work, enabling them to take part in providing the tremendous needs of society and supporting Kingdom of God transformation around the world. Let's imagine a Kingdom Community which fosters exchanges of experience and ideas among the masses. Let's imagine a Kingdom Community which upholds and gives increasingly GOD given expression to cultural diversity in the media and arts and educational system, all in an atmosphere that brings out human community and commonality. Let's imagine GOD's Kingdom Community that provides forms of self-government and autonomy for the formerly oppressed nationalities, and provides resources that enable those autonomous areas to flourish, with vibrant educational and Kingdom cultural institutions and real self-government in other spheres...but which does not *require* people of those nationalities to live in such areas, and which promotes integration broadly throughout society.

Let's imagine a Kingdom Community that gives initiative to and backs up the people *combating* the racist, white supremacist ideas and ways of relating that will have been handed down from the old testament and new testament, a Kingdom Community that fosters the breaking down of barriers and exposing the false doctrines and hurtful myths that people have been taught about each other, and a Kingdom Community that—as opposed to today, when racism poison the airwaves—uses the media and schools to set a whole different atmosphere. Let's imagine this—and let's do more than just imagine. Let's *understand* that such things have been done where a Kingdom Community have taken place and exploited unrighteousness, or that we have learned more fully, through that experience, the need and importance of making these kinds of radical changes. And let's begin working to prepare for that Kingdom work, which would take the power out of the hands of the oppressors, and bring forth GOD's power & authority, in the hands of the masses, led by the Holy Spirit of GOD. In all this, the existence of GOD's Kingdom Community solid core that comes at everything as "emancipators of humanity" will be crucial. This solid core will need to anchor and guide the whole   cultural process, firmly drawing the links between every stage of struggle and the goal of GOD's will. Of course, this solid core is not a once-and-for-all, never-changing thing; it would be constantly developing and   going through changes at each stage of our lives. This core must begin to be forged, through the process of hastening and preparing for a Holy revolutionary situation, and then developed further—in a whole different context—in the situation where millions of people are rising up to seize the power & authority of GOD, and then further still and in a far greater way in the context of this Holy society, in which it will be a guiding principle, and something actively encouraged, that everyone who yearns for Holy emancipation should take up and concern themselves with the problems of the radical transformation of society as a whole.

A crucial part of carrying out this transformation is grasping clearly the centrality of abolishing all forms of national oppression as a cornerstone of achieving "The Kingdom Community"; and also crucial in all this is that all those motivated by wanting to see an end, at long last, to the brutal and seemingly unending forms of oppression of black people and other oppressed peoples, must increasingly grasp how this can only be achieved in the context of Holy emancipating all of humanity and moving human society towards "GOD's Kingdom Community". The social make-up today poses many different challenges than it did in the '60s. One big difference—the far greater predominance of the illegal economy in the inner cities today, and the corresponding dominance of the "code of the streets" and the "gangsta" thing. The kinds of hopes of the movement that inspired people in the 1960s seem distant to many of the youth of today—again, both because hopes for revolution and a radically different and better world were temporarily dashed *and* because even those hopes that were realized (the removal of some legal barriers,) proved unable to deal with the larger problems caused by the system. On one level, that makes it harder to mobilize many youth today in struggle against the system. But this also points to the need to go much deeper than any struggles of the past, no matter how inspiring, and to go far beyond their horizons and demands. As seen in regard to Katrina and the contradictions between African-Americans and Latinos, the righteous Kingdom Community will bring into being knowledge, understanding and wisdom that can deal with these problems, relatively quickly; the reality of this fact has to be brought out for masses of people in powerful and vivid ways, repeatedly, boldly and from many different angles—with examples that point to the killing contradictions that people face every day and that show, in a living way, how these contradictions can and will be dealt with in a radically different way, in accordance with the common interests of the masses of people, once the righteous Kingdom Community has established a position that embodies and furthers those interests. On another level, this makes it all the more important to struggle sharply with youth, and others, to get into the wisdom of GOD and draw out the aspirations for freedom which exist, but have been stomped on and nearly buried by this demonic system.

The challenge has to be made: get out of trying to make it in "the game" which this demonic system has given you to play and in which you'll never be more than a pawn, used against the very people you come from; get into something that can finally bring an end to the long dark night brought down on people by that system. Rupture with the kill or be killed mentality and the mind-set that comes with "the game"—and unleash what "the game" has suppressed: the aspirations for freedom and Holy emancipation for *all* people that have been buried but not killed…and the deep   desire to turn your anger and daring where, and against whom, it should and must be turned to realize *those* aspirations. Get out of seeking to get over on and even killing people just like you—and get into fighting the demonic powers today, as part of getting ready for this Holy revolution, and as part of transforming the people to make that Kingdom Community. There were glimpses of this potential in Hurricane Katrina, when people in "the life" sometimes risked all to save someone from a different "set," and in some of what happened in the 1992 L.A. Rebellion, when gang antagonisms were temporarily put to the side. There was more than a glimpse in the '60s, when people broke out of the criminal life and into the revolutionary movement. And there must be much more of that in the community today—brought forward by the righteous in Christ, and all who come to deeply understand that a radically different future is possible, with this becoming in turn a tremendous force of inspiration for millions more…*not* in some scheme to "stop the violence" that cannot work in this demonic system, and *not* in a gang truce that can never be more than a truce…but in a righteous Kingdom Community aiming to change everything. Yes, there are difficult challenges in building and maintaining GOD's Kingdom Community here on earth today. But to think that one can emancipate humanity without confronting challenges this tough and far tougher is to turn away from reality. And that we cannot do, and do not need to do. We have the tools to biblically understand the world and society, to figure out why things happen and how to change them, and to bring out of that a new world; we have to join together and use them. To be very clear: none of this will come easy. It will entail tremendous struggle and sacrifice, and it will only come about amidst great upheaval and even death and destruction—brought about largely by the forces seeking to keep in effect the old order of oppression and exploitation—which will of necessity be part of finally overthrowing and doing away with this demonic system upon Christ   return.

It will entail tremendous struggle and   sacrifice, and it will only come about amidst great upheaval and even death and destruction—brought about largely by the forces seeking to keep in effect the old order of oppression and exploitation—which will of necessity be part of finally overthrowing and doing away with this demonic system upon Christ return. But this struggle and sacrifice can, at long last, serve to completely sweep away the chains of oppression that have bound so many for so long, and bring about a true Holy emancipation. Such a righteous community would be greeted with joy in every corner of the world and inspire hundreds of millions, throughout the globe, to take up this cause that the "Kingdom Message" reach the four corners of the earth. Amen!!

CHAPTER VI

The Principle

Principle:

A **principle** is a <u>law</u> or <u>rule</u> that has to be, or usually is to be followed, or can be desirably followed, or is an inevitable consequence of something, such as the laws observed in nature or the way that a system is constructed. The principles of such a system are understood by its users as the essential characteristics of the system, or reflecting system's designed purpose, and the effective operation or use of which would be impossible if any one of the principles was to be ignored Indigent black men who wander the streets public places of towns and cities, stationing themselves as unwanted doormen at entrances to stores and cash machines, begging for money in train and bus stations, making pests of themselves as they accost the windshields of cars, foraging in trash cans, and begging from children. A seemingly endless stream of lost souls with time on their hands and no place to go. Are these men faced with the possibility of night riders bent on destroying whatever they create, as was S B Fuller, in the 1930s Louisiana, who came close to a face-off with the Klan, yet went on to establish and expand his phenomenally successful Fuller Products, which eventually employed hundreds of blacks across the country? Are these men living under the burden of oppressive Jim Crow Legislation as did Henry Allen Boyd who, nevertheless, in the 20s, developed one business after another in Nashville. Founded a bank to provide capital for other entrepreneurs, all the while working to reform racist laws?

Surely, today's drifters need not be fearful of amassing capital lest it be snatched from them, a possibility that must have worried William Pettiford who, nonetheless, in 1899, as head of the Alabama Penny Loan and Savings Bank, provided loans to his fellow blacks, a task that gave him great pride and satisfaction. How did the men who are today's vagabonds become so bereft of a sense of mission, if only for themselves? How is it that most of them have no knowledge of the black men who, long before America's official slavery ended, long before anything called an Emancipation Proclamation, had the confidence to make the most of their free status and sustained their families in dignity? What force of circumstance so totally cut off today's derelicts from that tradition of blacks who would have preferred to die rather than be viewed as anything except as "credit to the race?"The very real restrictions on black economic mobility in the past have been reencountered in many sources. A Historian describes the mass of legislation, especially in the South, that was designed to limit the black man's ability to effectively compete in the marketplace with whites. Such laws forced blacks into what was called an "economic detour", as they attempted, like members of all other groups, to create economic foundations thru business enterprise. Biased laws denied them the ability to expand their enterprises beyond the borders of black communities. Yet, in spite of these "legal" maneuvers", over the generations, tens of thousands of black men mastered the economic principles that drove American society. Under the guidance and encouragement of leaders like Booker T Washington, a great many managed to prosper even within a limited economic niche. Butler reports that between 1867 and 1917, the number of black-owned businesses INCREASED from 4,000 to 50,000!All this business activity is evidence of the family bonds that were strongly in place as brothers, sisters, cousins, uncles and offspring worked together to maintain the family businesses. In economist studies, which cite the critical importance of TRUST among members of various immigrant groups, as they re-establish their lives in new countries, pooling resources and putting off immediate pleasures. It is claimed that a sense of trust among members is the key to any group's future progress.

Among blacks, in this early period, the examples of familial cooperation are legion. Pretentious "Intellectuals" Yet, all the while that blacks were experiencing varying degrees of success as craftsman, farmers, business proprietors, and even as founders of towns in the South and Southwest, a growing number of "intellectuals" in the North were shaping agendas that eventually would re-direct the attention of the masses. More formally educated than most blacks and eager to enjoy life's comforts, their driving ambitions centered primarily around the trappings of success. In the 1850s, an abolitionist described freed blacks who yearned for prestigious occupations. He exhorted them 1st to emulate others who understood the necessity of educating their children "to do everyday practical business." Such people were wise, because they were willing to take one step at a time. Living in a period prior to the imposition of severe legal restrictions on black enterprise, "This has been one of our great mistakes we have gone in advance of ourselves. We have commenced at the superstructure of the building, instead of the foundation at the top instead of the bottom. We should 1st be mechanics and common tradesmen, and professions as a matter of course would grow out of the wealth made there by "founded a bank to provide capital for other entrepreneurs, all the while working to reform racist laws? Surely, today's drifters need not be fearful of amassing capital lest it be snatched from them, a possibility that must have worried William Pettiford who, nonetheless, in 1899, as head of the Alabama Penny Loan and Savings Bank, provided loans to his fellow blacks, a task that gave him great pride and satisfaction. How did the men who are today's vagabonds become so bereft of a sense of mission, if only for themselves? How is it that most of them have no knowledge of the black men who, long before America's official slavery ended, long before anything called an Emancipation Proclamation, had the confidence to make the most of their free status and sustained their families in dignity?

What force of circumstance so totally cut off today's derelicts from that tradition of blacks who would have preferred to die rather than be viewed as anything except as "credit to the race?" The very real restrictions on black economic mobility in the past have been reencountered in many sources. A Historian describes the mass of legislation, especially in the South, that was designed to limit the black man's ability to effectively compete in the marketplace with whites. Such laws forced blacks into what was called an "economic detour", as they attempted, like members of all other groups, to create economic foundations thru business enterprise. Biased laws denied them the ability to expand their enterprises beyond the borders of black communities. Yet, in spite of these "legal" maneuvers", over the generations, tens of thousands of black men mastered the economic principles that drove American society. Under the guidance and encouragement of leaders like Booker T Washington, a great many managed to prosper even with in a limited economic niche. Butler reports that between 1867 and 1917, the number of black-owned businesses INCREASED from 4,000 to 50,000! All this business activity is evidence of the family bonds that were strongly in place as brothers, sisters, cousins, uncles and offspring worked together to maintain the family businesses. In economist studies which cites the critical importance of TRUST among members of various immigrant groups, as they re-establish their lives in new countries, pooling resources and putting off immediate pleasures. It is claimed that a sense of trust among members is the key to any group's future progress. Among blacks, in this early period, the examples of familial cooperation are legion. Pretentious "Intellectuals" This was the course that would be followed in the early part of this century by the Tuskegee-inspired southern blacks. It was warned that those who would have blacks "leap too far" encouraged the young to possess either no "qualification at all, or a collegiate education," leaping from the deepest abyss to the highest summit, "without medium or intermission. But the black elites were to take their lead from a band of white liberals and other black "scholars" and pendants, led principally by W. E. B. DuBois, a man who, by 1890, had achieved a doctorate from Harvard University. He was to play a major role in attempts to undermine Tuskegee's outstanding success with the poorest blacks. DuBois dismissed as unworthy the labor of craftsmen, farmers and business owners. In his zeal, he talked of "turning carpenters into men".

For, in that peculiar world into which he had assimilated, one who labored or was bereft of a college degree could hardly be considered a man (at least in DuBois' eyes,). It is this pretentious spirit that was to become the hallmark of the black elite (and still exist today seeing DuBois is the "father" of the NAACP leadership, and others who follow this philosophy of elitism); whose over riding influence would shape the thinking and behavior of future generations of blacks. DuBois set out to convince the masses that they shared the same interests as the elite. It became clear to this cynical crew, who were already actively soliciting whites for greater political and social interaction, that success would be more likely if such demands were made in the name of the entire race, not just affluent, educated gentry. Corrupting the Work Ethic. Among blacks, the undiluted pretentions of this elite was legendary and had already become the stuff of mockery and ridicule, long before it was chronicled in the 40s and 50s by blacks From earliest times, it is members of this elite, more concerned with image and immediate gratification than with the task of building, who have sent forth signals that have contributed to undermining the work ethic among the poor. Zealous in their own desires to avoid the prospect of menial labor, they encouraged the poor to disdain "dead end jobs and to hold out for meaningful work". (Now the point here is not to slam our community for our lack of training, which may be one major reason for denial of higher paying wages, but it is setting a mental block that certain jobs are to be refused because "they don't pay enough." But if the job market has nothing else to offer, what are we to do? And remember, our parents would take whatever job they could find to put food on our tables. This work ethic is not there today.) On a practical level, the unemployed poor also play important roles as symbols. Held as hostages in the war against "the system", they can be publicly displayed as more victims of "racism", a situation best dealt with by devising more and more social programs (many which are doomed to fail before they get out of the gate because of gross mismanagement and an inept bureaucracy feeding off of the poverty they are supposed to "cure). The message of the elite has taken firm root in the culture of the poor.

In a 1989 interview, George Waters, director of EDTEC, an organization in Camden, NJ, that teaches entrepreneurial skills to youth, described the greatest obstacle to youngsters' success as "attitude". Waters said, We're up against unproductive attitudes toward work, which have been instilled into these youngsters, not only by their peers on the streets, but also by parents who actually tell their kids that working for fast food wages is beneath them. Here is a big problem. Many poor kids whose parents may be on welfare, for example, may not have employable skills. But they want the better things of society, and may not be willing to work for them. So a kid thinks it's better to take an easier route to gets these material items. It's the wanting of material goods which becomes the goal in the minds of the kids and not realizing one has to prepare oneself with skills via education and studying for a job in the open job market assuming they are there. Quite naturally, hustling and drug sales provide the ends but the means are devastating to our community. There are adults who actually pass such notions on to kids." In another era, before the corrupt views of the elite achieved dominance, the humblest blacks believed what Sowell teaches, that there is no such things as a dead end job-which it is up to the individual to turn every work experience into a chance to either learn skills, or improve work habits, or position oneself for achieving still higher goals. In interviews, members of today's black elite make clear that even Mom and Pop ventures are to be avoided, since they are not "viable" businesses that can produce the high incomes to which they would like to become accustomed. Busy as members of this class are with trying to break thru those glass ceilings in white corporations, in their quest for higher level positions, they cannot summon the concern to help those on the lowest rungs find the economic means to create these smaller enterprises.

A publication from a black Washington, DC "think tank" offers a brief historical survey of American black business, and then condescendingly dismisses the many small businesses that were formed. The article laments that, "The blacks who were lured into the world of business in the 20s were typically not the ones who were highly educated", and goes on to imply that since such businesses were not created by the more affluent and did not grow beyond a limited size, they were hardly worth noting. Those thousands of black-owned businesses that were created by the humblest people and had sustained families and employed children were not the "viable" kind that would be acceptable to the needs of the better classes. Parasites on the Poor, after last year's riots in LA, it was no surprise that middle class blacks closed ranks around the vandals and explained away the roots of the rioting with the tired old charges of "societal neglect". This was a sure way to deflect those taboo questions from being asked of them: "What are you people doing about the mess in the black community?" and "Where is the input of the middle class? other than as apologists and makers of excuses for inexcusable acts." Both these questions are relevant seeing South Central LA has deteriorated over the past 30 years. What have our "leaders" been doing during this time? It's been 40 years since the Watts riots and the situation in South Central LA hasn't improved that much other than a former Mayors holding an office for much of that time, with nothing being accomplished. They've been benefitting from the social programs they have managed which supposed to work for the benefit of the people. Those are questions you can be certain that members of the friendly liberal media will never ask. A sociologist writes, "Members of the black middle class essentially occupy a parasitic relationship to the black underclass." Consumed primarily with a quest for recognition and validation, they derive satisfaction only to the degree that the white world grants them "here a news anchor (jobs), there a distributorship."

TV journalist Tony Brown, his syndicated column, regularly speaks direct toward members of this class for neglecting to take up their responsibility to lead with their money, instead of with rhetoric and bluster. He views their indifferences the true waste in the black community. Brown claims that the only role played by middle class is as "managers of resources allocated by government and corporate programs." They are, in effect, overseers of the bounty. He charges them with acknowledging a connection to their race, in order to "pick up their affirmative action paychecks." This is an acknowledgement of these "overseers" as being the primary beneficiaries of these social programs, not the people they claim they are serving. A disproportionate number of these elites shamelessly earn their livings directly off the adversities of the poor. Are black men shooting one another down in the streets and filling up the prisons across the land? Are black teens irresponsibly producing babies....? Members of the middle class view such tragedy as "opportunities" for personal advancement. For every demonstration of pathology offers the chance to submit "proposals" for yet newer and trendier social programs that will, of course require the input of the elites' wise and judicious expertise. In fact, each tragedy in our community has its own armies of social workers eager to verify their nebulous theories about our behavior. Our "leaders" conveniently "volunteer" our participation with these experts so they can collect their reward. Black social problems offer unlimited ideas for workshop topics and themes for the endless string of conferences funded by the Philip Morris and Anheuser-Busches and hosted by the growing numbers of black social scientists and talk circuit riders. No group understood the self-interest and hypocrisy of the elite better than the militants, the self-proclaimed black nationalists. More connected to the grassroots, thru out the 60s the militants publicly confronted and badgered the black middle class for their exploitative role. Loud and belligerent, militants promoted racial solidarity, while threatening to hold the "sell-out social class" accountable for their indifference to the real needs of the poor. If any group stood a chance to rallying the poor to take initiatives in their own behalf, the down-home, no-nonsense militants might have pulled it off. Invoking the rhetoric of Marcus Garvey's self-help movement, they talked a powerful line.

However, the militant's role was soon diminished during the latter part of the 60s and early 70s. In fact, their role become one of a joke, laughed to scorn as they were not taken seriously no more. What happened? Anybody remember James Brown's song "Talkin' Loud and Sayin' Nothing? Well, the militants were doing a lot of loud talking, and little action to back up the talk. And they talked and talked, and talked. People got tired of their talk with no action to back it up. Except for the few who were to make national headlines for varying forms of violence, talking is just about all they did. As media promotion turned many of them into instant celebrities, some became heady in the limelight. Now the elite also exploited tactics used by the militants to make it more appealing to the "grassroots". Many "Black leaders" immediately picked up on this tactic and became the "spokesmen" for our community. The liberal media also helped by promoting their faces in the public's eye so much even we have accepted their "leadership" and played along with the act. It was not long before the world was witness to their hypocrisy. For when the government money began pouring in to pay for Great Society programs, the militants beat the social class to the head of the line to cash in. They proved to be as imaginative as the rest of the pack in devising worthless but lucrative social programs. Lacking an iota of sincerity, and caught up as they were in the trappings of foolishness, they proved to be yet another faction who viewed the black poor as personal property, ripe for the picking. As had been pointed out in several candid works by blacks, an attachment to socialist principles has proven a comfortable cop-out for a great many black men-providing a rationale for the ongoing expression of anger at the so called white man's "system, and alibis for not becoming active economic competitors. The fear of failure has made many fall prey to the seduction of the political left. The story of "The Endangered Black Family", discusses the tension that such defenses create, claiming that at the heart of the discord between many black men and women is the woman's suspicion that, "the black man's chant is but an unconscious evasion for his own incompetence and reluctance to contend in the marketplace." the fact that the vitality of this agony man is spent on what he calls the "dream-scheme complex", a mental fantasyland that prevents him from dedicating his energies to the "necessary day-to-day endeavors in the mundane world." Eventually scorned by others, his defensive posturing only increases, "in such a way as to externalize every portion of the responsibility for his fate far away from himself."

Today's' militant has transformed himself from the Marxist to "Afro-centrist", and although our current militants has hitched a socialist wagon to an Afro-centrist start, the message he spouts makes it clear that his Chieftain is still none other than old Uncle Pete decked out in Kente cloth. One could call it blasphemous that, almost to a man, these militants pay homage to Marcus Garvey, making claim to his strong nationalist teachings. Every year, they come on his birthday and other occasions to celebrate their patron saint. Yet, there was no greater advocate of capitalism than Garvey. Not only did he show blacks, by example, how to access the economic system, he taught that capitalism was the best route to prosperity for the "little man." He abhorred all forms of collectivist schemes, claiming that communism "robs the individual of his personal initiative and ambition or the result thereof." There is ample proof of this by witnessing the fall of communism in Eastern Europe all with the former Soviet Union. In more practical terms, the examples of how socialist welfare programs rob our own people of their initiatives, while our "leaders" become the prime benefactors of our condition. Marcus Garvey strictly denounced Communism and their socialist theories as a solon to our plight. In fact, during the 30s a large number of his confrontations were with "black" communists who believed in socialists ideals. Garvey saw thru the communists game of using our community to further their own objectives, as many other liberal types still do today, and not really caring about our overall condition in the United States. *Not for Garvey the depiction of poverty as a morally superior state or condition. On the contrary, he indicated that a man who remained poor was evidence of someone who had failed to make the most of his abilities and world's opportunities.* The nationalism of yesterday's militant or today's Afro-centrist is without focus or base. Garvey's brand of nationalism had an economic mooring and purpose, and it gave his followers constructive goals towards which to work. Garveyites were to be "up and doing," they were to be achievers.

Those black men of that earlier period of our history, who took the lead in the entrepreneurial activities, were looked upon as the natural authority figures in their communities, held in regard by their peers and respected by the young. After citing the all too well-known statistics that show single men of all groups as more prone to mental and chronic diseases and the perpetrators of most crime, the manner in which American social policy, most of which no longer reinforces the family, consequently induces men to disrupt rather than support society. As historical fact and as common sense, it once was accepted wisdom that the major reason for the institution of marriage, which assures a man's union to a woman, was to help put brakes on men's aggressiveness to turn their focus away intemperate self-indulgence toward more responsible behavior. The claim that when normal socializing restraints are no longer in place and the social institutions deny the basic terms of male nature, "Masculinity makes men enemies of family and society." And where a welfare bureaucracy has entirely replaced their economic function, men are even less likely to play positive roles in the ongoing sustenance of communities. What a strange coincidence with our condition today. Very prophetic insight..... As feminists and homosexuals increasingly influence the making of public policy, they are helping to establish directives and laws that are detrimental to family cohesiveness. Can we soon expect to see changes in the behavior of young men of other groups who, in   growing numbers, will begin to duplicate the hostile patterns of the young black male? As is clear from the study of all groups, as well as those earlier "segregated" black communities, where married men function as husbands and fathers, it is they who set the tone and influence the nature of the community. Among blacks, where almost 60% of men are single "rolling stones", it is they who set the tone in ghetto neighborhoods. Author Jawanza Kunjufu speculates that, "By the year 2000, 70% of all black males will be unavailable to black women- in gangs, unemployed or on drugs." Its 2014 and that trend is something many black women can verify right now. Also in recent years, some hate literature from a skin-head group claiming it is the plan of these hate-groups to "eliminate" our population by our men's participation in rolling stone life-style vagabonds, gang members, or homosexuals not that they control our behavior, but we are certainly making their job a lot easier.

In fact, it would not be surprise if many of these hate-groups are behind the trafficking of illegal drugs decimating our community. Such men cannot or will not be worthy for many sisters as future husbands. Such men cannot or will not be worthy for many sisters as future husbands. This number also includes those who are in prisons. And, might we add still in Stanley Crouch's opinion) another possible loss, given the advent of school curricula that glamorize homosexuality.... (in the name of tolerance?). Such curricula are already underway in many major city public schools now. And with the backing the teaching of such moral falsehood? -That's right. The NAACP has backed and "endorsed" such curricula at least; the leadership of the organization has because the members have not had the opportunity to express their opinion on it seeing last July's meeting had this issue censored by said leadership. Whether or not the NAACP leadership is challenged on this still remains to be seen. The last delegate meeting showed the "leaders" reluctance to discuss the issue with the overall body. How long do they think they can continue to do that, and claim to be our "spokesmen and women"? It's just a matter of time when more members will leave the NAACP because of the "leaders" refusal to listen to its membership. In fact, this is happening already, now that some "conservative blacks" are having their viewpoints heard publicly. Is there will be a plan to "silence" these "conservatives". Watch out for future propaganda side shows as both sides try to line up their views to confront one another. Does this mean "disunity" within the house of our community? No. But as the "Word of GOD" says in the end every knee shall bow. The NAACP-type groups have allowed their   viewpoints to be the only "official" viewpoint. It's, therefore, of no coincidence that they have received the media backing from liberal white press. "Conservative" blacks as a term should be irrelevant anyway. We need to use a common- sense approach to deal with our problems. Many times there is no need for a political front which the NAACP or their leadership, wishes to put everything on. And as "conservative" blacks make this known, they are slammed as UNCLE TOM'S. This occurred in one of the issues of Emerge magazine. Ben Chavis gave his "version" of a delegate meeting where objections were heard. He had an interview with a reporter from the magazine; but he never discussed why some delegates who he calls "right-wing reactionaries" wanted an explanation for the NAACPs association of Homosexual causes to be equivalent to the black civil rights, which is what cause the "disruption" to begin with.

In fact, it would not be surprise if many of these hate-groups are behind the trafficking of illegal drugs decimating our community. Such men cannot or will not be worthy for many sisters as future husbands. Such men cannot or will not be worthy for many sisters as future husbands. This number also includes those who are in prisons. And, might we add still in Stanley Crouch's opinion) another possible loss, given the advent of school curricula that glamorize homosexuality.... (in the name of tolerance?). Such curricula are already underway in many major city public schools now. And with the backing the teaching of such moral falsehood? -That's right. The NAACP has backed and "endorsed" such curricula at least; the leadership of the organization has because the members have not had the opportunity to express their opinion on it seeing last July's meeting had this issue censored by said leadership. Whether or not the NAACP leadership is challenged on this still remains to be seen. The last delegate meeting showed the "leaders" reluctance to discuss the issue with the overall body. How long do they think they can continue to do that, and claim to be our "spokesmen and women"? It's just a matter of time when more members will leave the NAACP because of the "leaders" refusal to listen to its membership. In fact, this is happening already, now that some "conservative blacks" are having their viewpoints heard publicly. Is there will be a plan to "silence" these "conservatives". Watch out for future propaganda side shows as both sides try to line up their views to confront one another. Does this mean "disunity" within the house of our community? No. But as the "Word of GOD" says in the end every knee shall bow. The NAACP-type groups have allowed their viewpoints to be the only "official" viewpoint. It's, therefore, of no coincidence that they have received the media backing from liberal white press. "Conservative" blacks as a term should be irrelevant anyway. We need to use a common- sense approach to deal with our problems. Many times there is no need for a political front which the NAACP or their leadership, wishes to put everything on. And as "conservative" blacks make this known, they are slammed as UNCLE TOM'S. This occurred in one of the issues of Emerge magazine. Ben Chavis gave his "version" of a delegate meeting where objections were heard. He had an interview with a reporter from the magazine; but he never discussed why some delegates who he calls "right-wing reactionaries" wanted an explanation for the NAACPs association of Homosexual causes to be equivalent to the black civil rights, which is what cause the "disruption" to begin with.

The damage done by black intellectuals and later by white feminists, who undermined and eventually destroyed the credibility of the 65 Moynihan Report- a document of research and analysis that gravely warned of oncoming collapse of the black family. White feminists groups banned together in criticizing efforts of some Detroit blacks who wish to develop separate schools for the young black males in that city, as if they really care about any education our sons or daughters get. But, again, no rallying cries from the black elite to support the efforts of the schools to be formed in Detroit. Why? The report's urbane message emphasized the need for policies designed to strengthen the economic role of black men. Embarrassed by the frankness of the report and its bleak picture of abandoned women and children, defensive throngs of black academicians and other notables, along with pandering whites, worked to suppress the report's further distribution, and attacked its conclusions as "racist". "While black intellects with their condominiums and 2-car garages, continue to research out and assert the "strengths' of the black family, everywhere black people were crying the blues, as male-female conflict mounted and things continued to fall apart." Once again, interfering and opportunistic black elites, buttressed by whites, set agendas and, in effect, decided the fate of the black masses. By denying the severity of deep-seated patterns, they stood by as the black family continued to crumble. The experience of Black Americans should be instructive, to one, and all and for generations to come, as evidence of what happens when men give up their role of moral authority in the affairs of their own community. As black youngsters spin out of control, grasping at all wrong methods to attain the recognition that would be theirs in stable family life, they have become menaces even to themselves. Not only are wild, unruly boys failed by the adults, they learn early that black men, especially, haven't a clue about how to get a handle on the unremitting social decline. Many people do have answers, but the "mainstream leaders" want to make this a political affair so they can extort money for more government programs. The problem is the communities and it have to solve without much government intervention. But, as always, our "leaders" continue to believe going to government and throwing the problem at the government's feet is the way to go. Ideas which disagree with this approach are slammed especially if it challenges the "leaders" politics.

Remember "leaders" are the real beneficiaries of such programs while the masses are held hostage to their rhetoric and politics. Earlier in the year 1993, in Chicago, a group of black men participated in a series of so-called summit meetings with members of street gangs. The gang leaders were encouraged to declare "truces" to limit their turf "wars" on the community. They signed, along with neighborhood dignitaries, documents called "peace treaties". All of this formal ceremony took place, as the youth were treated as diplomats or "heads of state". Meanwhile, in another city, a group of black men aiming to stem local violence formed a "rap" group appropriating the children's own symbols of rebellion. This was done, they explained, so they might better "relate" to the youth. And similar antics are being duplicated in cities around the country. Now no one is effectively slamming these efforts to get gang members to understand that violence has no place in the community. In fact, such efforts should always encourage. But, rather, it's the timing and political propaganda undertones which should concern all people. Our communities have been steadily becoming more violent in the past 30 years or so. Why, now, have these "leaders" decided it is appropriate to "take a stand" against the violence? It was funny that many of these meetings were planned right after the LA riots in 1992. But, since then "where have our so call 'leaders' been the past 30 years?" The streets in our communities didn't just deteriorate overnight. So one may be inclined to believe an ulterior motive may be at work here. When Ben Chavis became the exec director of the NAACP, It was believed his main objective to put the NAACP "in the spotlight" of things concerning our community. No better way to do this than to "enlist" the help of street gangs by having it appears like they are really doing something for the community. But this attempt was 30 years too late. Did these street gang members have any say in political matters of the NAACP? Doubt it. During a delegate meeting of the NAACP, regular members were upset because they were left out of the decision making process concerning the supporting of homosexual rights and the association of the black struggle and the homosexual community, in general. It was naive then to think our brother Ben Chavis, and others were really concerned about the gangs? 30 years of neglect by our "leaders" have occurred?

The easy answer to the question would probably be Ben Chavis saying something like "the NAACPs leadership has gone thru a change at that time and rightfully so it has, and they are more 'caring' now. When Ben Chavis became the exec director of the NAACP, It was believed his main objective to put the NAACP "in the spotlight" of things concerning our community. No better way to do this than to "enlist" the help of street gangs by having it appears like they are really doing something for the community. But this attempt was 30 years too late. Did these street gang members have any say in political matters of the NAACP? Doubt it. During a delegate meeting of the NAACP, regular members were upset because they were left out of the decision making process concerning the supporting of homosexual rights and the association of the black struggle and the homosexual community, in general. It was naive then to think our brother Ben Chavis, and others were really concerned about the gangs? 30 years of neglect by our "leaders" have occurred? The easy answer to the question would probably be Ben Chavis saying something like "the NAACPs leadership has gone thru a change at that time and rightfully so it has, and they are more 'caring' now. What a demonstrations could there be of the NAACPs total failure as a moral voice. Here are wayward boys who, at the very least, need to have their ears boxed, and at the most, ought to be disciplined and punished by tough, caring men. Instead, it is the boys who have the upper hand and call the shots in the new-found self- importance, while making their elders look like fools. The examples or roles models of fathers is crucial here. We all are aware that there are many fatherless homes in our community. The role of men is very important in setting the direction for the community. Now this does not downplay the role of mothers- many who have to be both mother and father because a young child's father fled the scene for whatever reason. Young boys without the guidance, therefore, seek to make their own role models with gang membership, drug selling, and other activities which bring devastation to our community. Are we to expect women to wear the responsibility that we, men, have decided to forfeit? Public schools are indoctrinating our son's with homosexual curricula... in the name of tolerance. What aspect of black manhood do our sons have to look forward to? Our roles are, therefore, very important. And no government or social programs can replace the importance of fathers providing moral guidance for their families.

Worse, such accommodating behavior on the part of adults send clear signals to black youth, who find fewer men to respect, that they will be rewarded after committing even the most heinous offenses. These boys are without fathers, grandfathers or uncles, to observe and emulate, and the men whose tactics are recounted above do nothing to increase their youthful regard for black men. Where can any community expect to end up when the masses of its men no longer command the respect of its sons? When most of its youth grow to perceive male authority as hollow and feeble and, often, even laughable? Black Men Were Producers Not men cited in no position to offer any economic alternatives to these boys, because THEY HAVE CREATED NOTHING OF ECONOMIC VALUE. Most who participated in the "treaty" signings were church pastors; others described themselves as "community activists". Not one in a position to take a boy under his wing and offer him a job. Such was not always the case among the black community. The sons of Isaiah Montgomery, for example, knew the power of a father's authority, as they watched him and relatives, in the late 1880s; carve the town of Mound Bayou, Ms, out of a wilderness. So did the sons of businessmen Philip Payton, George Whitelaw Lewis, John Merrick, Joseph Lee, William Pettiford, John Mitchell, S.B. Fuller and countless others whose names are lost in history. Not to mention Booker T. Washington, who built Tuskegee Institute with nothing other than a hand full of change in his pocket. Tuskegee Institute is now one of the finest AA Universities in the country. So did the sons of farmers and craftsmen and cooks and butlers. These men were not confused about the roles they were obligated to play in the protection and sustenance of their families. This shows we have numerous examples of builders within our own history to use as examples. But do we really KNOW our history? And this does not infer we blame whites for not teaching us our history- which some black people do sometimes. Clearly we've lost the legacy and work ethic our ancestors had at striving to build better lives for their families and their community. Historical events have clearly made our people a collective body in many ways. And today, we are allowing a large number of young black men; possibly destroy our future because of lack of guidance. But should we look to the government via social agencies, or the majority society to provide that guidance? NO! Those businessmen among them took risks using their money and expertise to develop the communities in which they lived, even during the worst days of hostility toward our race.

They did so not because it was considered "courageous" thing to do, but because this is what was expected of them, this is what men did. And the boys watched and learned, form what they saw, and knew what would be expected of them one day. They saw black men as creators, producers and initiators of opportunities, instead of as passive agents awaiting some inevitable fate. What happened to bring about this long-lost legacy? Escape to the Church, King Solomon of Ecclesiastes asks, "For whom am I toiling and depriving myself of pleasure?" Our black men once have a ready answer to that question. If so many of them no longer know how to answer this question, it might very well be due to the legacy of the Civil Rights movement and stratagems that have been forcefully transmitted by the black church for the past 30 years. Few institutions in this country have a nobler image than the black church. Endlessly praised for its early role in an antagonistic world, it is generally considered off limits to close inspection or criticism. Now look at the black church's role in our community development. The points here are not directed to all churches. Churches play an immensely important role in the spiritual   development of any community. But what happens when churches don't live up to their role. However God is no respecter of persons. He loves us all and sent Christ to die for our sins too. When the Kingdom Message is not being portrayed by our churches, then what use do they have to us? Many people in our community, quite naturally, shun away from the church because of "hypocrites" they see claiming to be Christians. The example they see are "preachers" who are not living up to the standard Christians or ministers of the Faith are supposed to be. However, later on in life, the meaning behind the Message is "Salvation thru Christ". And it has nothing to do with skin color or political persuasion. Many churches are not delivering that message, and they have God to deal with for not living up to their responsibility. It was not off limits, however, in the early 1900s, to Booker T Washington's piercing scrutiny. In fact, one of the reasons why Washington was resented by the elites of his day was the laser like probe he turned on the various hypocrisies of certain blacks, and his no nonsense assessment of them. When it came to the disproportionate numbers of black men who became "preachers" or took to politics for a living, he could be merciless in his criticism.

He publicly lamented the loss to the race of its most vigorous and ambitious men, who chose these easier paths to esteem and financial support. Washington claimed that as soon as some black men "halfway learn to read and write," they grabbed a Bible and ran to an open a church or they took to a political stump. Or they did both. It should be pointed out that not everyone can "become" a preacher. 1). one has to have the highest moral codes to live by to set an example for community members to emulate. This is more for spiritual character they are to be for the rest of us, at large. 2). one's devotion to God and His Will has to be the main motivating factor. Do we see this in large numbers from many churches within our community? Totally, probably not, Washington viewed this behavior as setting a precedent that could ultimately weaken the race. For, instead, of   playing economically productive roles, as did their counterparts such men removed themselves from the critical task of economic development. As solo operators, and heads of their own little private constituency of loyal followers, they could confidently look forward to some degree of prestige and dependable income. One has to wonder why churches are the only real institution which thrives in our community. There can be many reasons for this, but one reason is many feel "called" to become preachers. There are some churches where the leaders are of impeccable quality, but there are many who are not. In many cases such men are not inspired by God to preach. One should not take it up- on one's self to be a preacher. There is a difference. How is the everyday person to know this difference? Jesus said, "...by their fruits, you will know them....." Washington decried this "escape to the church", which usually included some heroic notions about finding grand solutions to the race problem. He was alarmed by the fact that the minds of a great many blacks were so "filled with the traditions of anti-slavery struggle," that it prevented them from "preparing for any definite task in the world." Instead, he complained large numbers fixed on the idea of "preparing themselves to solve the race problem." Because of the tradition of riding the circuit to preach abolition, there was already a strong tendency among many black men to view themselves as heirs to the great abolitionists, such as Frederick Douglass, and emulate these figures as a route to glory and prominence. So right here, the motivation is wrong to be called a Man of God.

Glory and prominence are the last things on the mind of a man convicted with the right spiritual insight he receives. And, again, one may see how some did not want to toil and strive thru hard work for the race. Rather, some decided becoming a preacher was a lot easier. But without conviction and dedication, many churches only become a bldg with 4 walls and a personal oasis for the pastor of the local flock. Over the years, Washington developed friendships with numbers of black ministers, several of whom he admired and respected. But that did not cloud his judgment about what was really at the bottom of why so many men chose this profession, (and still do today) this "safe haven" away from the competition. One year, when he was on a train ride from Alabama to Washington, DC, his train was boarded by a couple of dozen of black preachers who, apparently, were on the way to the capital for a church convention. They filled the car w/ laughter and high spirits, as they dined on home lunches smoked, played cards, drank bootleg liquor, and engaged in telling the course, off-color jokes. In observing their behavior and listening to their conversation, it struck Washington that "almost anybody who took a mind to it" could be a preacher. He was reminded of a joke about a poor farmer them making the rounds. It seems that the farmer, after spending years w/ his mule plowing hard, unyielding soiling the hot sun for long hrs every day, decided he had had enough if such labor. One day he put down his plow and looked to the sky and proclaimed, "Oh God, this sun is so hot, and this ground so hard, I do believe this Negro is called to preach." Could it be our misfortune that, almost a century later, so many black men are still dropping the plow (for economic development) and hearing the "call" to preach? (So right here, the motivation is wrong to be called a Man of God. Glory and prominence are the last things on the mind of a man convicted w/ the right spiritual insight he receives. And, again, one may see how some did not want to toil and strive thru hard work for the race. Rather, some decided becoming a preacher was a lot easier. But w/out conviction and dedication, many churches only become a bldg w/ 4 walls, and a personal oasis for the pastor of the local flock.) Over the years, Washington developed friendships w/ numbers of black ministers, several of whom he admired and respected. But that did not cloud his judgment about what was really at the bottom of why so many men chose this profession, (and still do today) this "safe haven" away from the competition.

One year, when he was on a train ride from Alabama to Washington, DC, his train was boarded by a couple of dozen of black preachers who, apparently, were on the way to the capital for a church convention. They filled the car w/ laughter and high spirits, as they dined on home lunches smoked, played cards, drank bootleg liquor, and engaged in telling the course, off-color jokes. In observing their behavior and listening to their conversation, it struck Washington that "almost anybody who took a mind to it" could be a preacher. He was reminded of a joke about a poor farmer them making the rounds. It seems that the farmer, after spending years w/ his mule plowing hard, unyielding soiling the hot sun for long hrs every day, decided he had had enough if such labor. One day he put down his plow and looked to the sky and proclaimed, "Oh God, this sun is so hot, and this ground so hard, I do believe this Negro is called to preach." Could it be our misfortune that, almost a century later, so many black men are still dropping the plow for economic development and hearing the "call" to preach? About how some preachers in churches in our community have abused their position. A good number of these ministers are concerned about the size of their church and whether or not all the seats are filled in the building. Even sometimes a minister's success is judged by the size of his church and the number of members attending the church. This is not the reason men are called to become preachers. A "Righteous Man of God" is more concerned about the spiritual matters that surround his community. He does have a responsibility to his "flock", but he is not concerned about the glamorous aspects of his ministry. His priorities are set by the following: God is number one in his life; 2). comes his family responsibility, 3). is his ministry, and 4th, 5th, 6th would probably be politics if he has the time left to tackle these problems. In some churches, the reverse may have happened. Because of charges of neglect of our community, many ministers take on politics. There are 2-3 reasons for doing this. One, there may be a genuine need to help the community; said ministers may feel a need to "increase his sphere of influence" In which many preachers appear to be more comfortable with their faces in the limelight. They may appear there so much, it becomes a battle to find new "causes" to have people believe they are helping the community. How many of our "leaders" are traditionally from the pulpit. ..

But a real leader, confident in himself, quietly builds behinds the scenes not creating a notice to himself. Such a leader refrains from the limelight, and really spends his self getting our people involved in doing things to take charge of their lives. They don't believe one should waste a lifetime blaming white folk for all of our problems. We have to deal with these, and we need to do what is best to alleviate the effects of them on us and our children which follow behind us. Do we have men with these virtues? Yes. Men like Rev. Anthony Martin and his organization helping our people become competitors in building businesses and creating jobs for themselves and their respective communities, is just one to serve as an example. My organization (GMI) called GM Interprise Inc is showing ordinary street folk what is necessary to take charge of their lives; how to create businesses and employ themselves, etc. Continuing on the line of virtues a leader has, is he/she may or may not be of a charmistic personality. Such personality traits are irrelevant because these people are more concerned about doing, rather than talking. Many of our "leaders" do the exact opposite. By loud talking, they seek to do whatever is necessary to tell people what they want to hear. They don't tell them or show by example what is necessary to change our predicament in this country. It is easy to understand, therefore, what the lyrics behind James Brown's: Talkin' Loud and Sayin' Nothing song is all about. Like many of our black leaders and preachers who bask in the limelight of media coverage. They offer no stratagems for creating a competitive edge in our community. No. They do the opposite having us continue to go to government with our hands out. This is certainly not the legacy the "Ancient of Days" had in mind. Certainly not what He would like to see us continue on earth. Why is it that we have drifted away from the "Righteous Ways of GOD? And How do we ever so turn back to the "Righteous Ways of GOD? Perhaps reliance on the Civil Rights movement too much convinced us the problems would be solved. We all know this is not true. 30 or 40 years later, and we are still struggling as hard as ever.

We've made some successes in getting black politicians elected, but we haven't advanced much on the economic front as a collective body. Going to the government won't do this, seeing that many social agencies usually control the lives of the individuals it is trying to help. Therefore a new strategy is needed to focus our community on economic development. The ideas of self-reliance have always been proven to be those which work. And we have examples of such within our history which may have been forgotten. Black preachers are numerous and everywhere. In some cities, black-owned newspapers fill several pages, not only with listings of all black churches in town along with each pastor's photo, but also with announcements of ordinations. In the 50s, sociologists discussed the question of whether the Negro population was "over churched". The subject is still as pertinent today. In terms of its most prominent and wealthiest members, Black Americans could be called "a race of athletes, entertainers, and preachers." A group with a miniscule number of entrepreneurs, it is understandable why its members are totally dependent on others for   employment. From early on, there were blacks expressing the concern that every time a black man built a church, instead of a business, he established his own personal "cathedral of commerce," to benefit himself and few others. In recent years, it has been pointed out that if the same percentage of the country's Asian men were to take to the pulpit, the political stump, the basketball court, or the entertainment stage, the masses of Asians would find themselves on the bottom of the economic barrel. The same for the European Nations. The fact of Martin Luther King, Jr. singular success as a heralded preacher plays so small part in the decisions of men to enter his profession. In an earlier period, the abolitionist was to be emulated; today is the civil rights leader. The precedent set by King to downplay the importance of economic independence, as he pushed for integration into white institutions, is fundamental to the ongoing decline of black masses. Despite the sometimes intense differences of opinion among blacks over the books on black men and women, has correctly assessed the implications of King's legacy. It was charged that King's very agenda, that is, encouraging blacks to take the final steps to dismantle all that we had built together, has "ended up being the very foundation of the problems blacks face today." In a stinging appraisal of King's message, it was pointed out a number of reasons why King makes a poor role model for today's young black men.

Since the King movement was defined by whites as "non-violent," those who opposed his strategies were viewed as possibly being for violence. However, many opposed King for his promotion of what historian call "non-economic liberalism." A researcher's op-ed article describes King, speaking before a group of whites in the 60s, sounding almost apologetic. As if to reassure his white audience that the drive for integration would not be deferred, he explained that it might be necessary to "temporarily" maintain some black businesses and schools "to prevent the loss of economic power that could result from complete integration." So, the Great Leader recognized that integration which meant the inevitable destruction of black cultural life an important unifying vehicle could mean the loss of economic power for his people. Yet he went on to drop the original call for desegregation and became integration's most persistent proponent. The question was, how much did he know or surmise and when did he know it? King Just Like Other Leaders Contrary to what some would have us believe, everything about King's public history indicates that he probably would be in support of much of civil rights policy that has transpired over the last 30 years- including the mass of affirmative action laws and biased quota stipulations. Eager to protect the Hero's image, King advocates prefer to believe that he would have taken routes different from those of the current opportunistic Civil Rights crew, most of whose efforts benefit black middle class. Citing King's call for the judging of individuals by the "content of their character," his champions claim that those who now wear his mantle would not have King's blessing. But the dubious and artificial role of "civil rights leader," a post to which no one gets elected Jessie Jackson conveniently assumed the reigns requires the constant nurturing of all kinds of bed fellows, if power is to be retained. Faced as Ben Chavis was with a withered   membership, when he took over the NAACP earlier in the year of 1993, King too probably would have been compelled to turn to manipulative interests groups such as feminists, homosexuals, and others, and to consort even with gang members, in efforts to expand his organizational base. As a faithful follower of the agendas set by white liberals, we would want to believe that King would not have joined with those who are responsible for encouraging the almost daily appearance of a new group of people who style themselves as "victims."

Unlike earlier black leaders, King helped to fix in the public mind the notion of blacks as victims. Also unlike earlier leaders, who had encouraged blacks to develop commerce among ourselves, King's mind set led him to scorn "big business," for the same reasons offered by various types of collectivists. , his preachments helped to make economic dependency a respectable option for blacks. Encouraging blacks to take economic initiatives. Why our community hasn't significantly made such progress economically with so many political "gains" we may have made. The answer is simple: we didn't develop the economic base to coincide with the politics. The examples of how politics work in this country: is based on money being the needed to make any politics work. Money which our community lacks because its "leaders" stiffen off of our own poverty, along with their liberal friends. A favorite saying among those who wish to rationalize male abandonment of families is a maxim attributed to Africa: "It takes a whole village to raise a child." In the context of the United States, what this really means is it takes the resources from the white folk's village (AFDC, welfare, food stamps, Medicaid, public housing) to raise the black man's child. Some of our more skilled cop-out artists claim that, in order to find solutions to black social problems, "We must take them to another level." This really means that we should divest ourselves of responsibility and turn them over to others. Such attitudes are reflected in two separate incidents during the 1992 Presidential campaign. At one of candidate Ross Perot's "town meetings," a black woman rose to ask his advice on how citizens might handle the crime and general mayhem that prevails in so many "minority" neighborhoods. Mr. Perot appeared momentarily perplexed. Could it be that he restrained himself from responding, "If you don't know what to do lady, how should I?" Ross Perot could have easily said something to that effect seeing his campaign style had a lot of one-liner quick sayings. However, he could not afford another embarrassing statement showing any insensitivity like before addressing black folk as "you people." The loss of male authority and guidance has exaggerated the role that politicians and other outsiders are expected to play, enlarging their powers among blacks. For blacks, politics has become a drug. . .

And when all problems are labeled "political," even the misbehavior of our children, one can expect to solve them only in the political arena. And this is where our "leaders" make financial gain. .Those closest to the problems is conveniently absolved of responsibility for finding solutions. And, by further claiming that all problems are "universal" and not particular, even men's abandonment of children, no personal responsibility should even be expected. The Cop-Outs In their zeal to offer excuses for their own inaction, black militants join with the middle class elites in standing truth on its head. For, whenever one of their excuses for failing to engage in economic competition is shown for the fraudulent cop-out it is, they set about contriving more elaborate ones. "We aspire much to a higher Afro-centrist ideal, unskilled by materialistic greed," "We are too noble to participate in the system that raped Africa and the 3rd World." While the Afro-centrist continues to expend their energy shouting obscenities at the good ol boy network or joining with the elites to extort some new quota-based perk, another industrious Asian buys a building on the block. It is a given that white and Asian men seem obligated to create jobs for black men. This may make one wonder why Koreans and Vietnamese have no respect for us. For, only members of these groups are expected to enlarge the economic pie. It is not even   suggested, for example, that the itinerant preachers, would do better by their race as the owner of a manufacturing plant that generates enough wealth to employ others. Nationalists like Martin Delany and Marcus Garvey never could have imagined the advantages blacks now possess. Such men surely would be stunned and dismayed at the opportunities squandered Imagine the different course we might now be on if, in the 60s Rap Brown, Stokely Carmichael, Eldridge Cleaver Bobby Seale and Huey Newton had been on fire to make manifest the economic strategies of Booker T Washington and Marcus Garvey-instead of resorting to angry debates in the symbolic dance with white folk. What might have come of a movement led by thousands of militant men who chose to put righteous indignation to work as builders, rather than as destroyers?

Of course, such fantasizing presupposes a militant mind set devoid of Marxist pretensions and free from the influence of white radicals. The militant shrewdly deduced, as did the followers of King, that confrontation with whites was the easier road to take than that of economic competition. Yet a nationalist idol of the militants long ago enjoined black men to take just the opposite course. "Let each one make the case his own and endeavor to rival his neighbor in honorable competition," intoned Martin Delany. Yet a nationalist idol of the militants long ago enjoined black men to take just the opposite course. "Let each one make the case his own and endeavor to rival his neighbor in honorable competition," intoned Martin Delany. After declaring that the means to develop manhood were within the reach of black men, he then asked, "Are we willing to try them?" Following the Liberals Black preachers, politicians and civil rights leaders form a strong protective circle. The politician support the civil rights defender, who, in turn, advances the agendas of the politician, and the preacher, from his pulpit, advances the causes of both. Black preachers can be notorious for their blind support of black politicians Remember those who rallied behind former DC mayor Marion Barry, who cried foul because he was a target of a sting operation by the FBI? The main question, again, here which was never asked by our "leaders" was: Why was he abusing his office and smoking cocaine to begin with? Instead, he was insulated from such cries by black politicians from the federal level and locally along with some preachers, and is often accused of acting as "fronts." All of these crusaders invoke the name of King and other civil rights martyrs, to remind blacks of the humiliations suffered to win the vote and to integrate white institutions. To be subservient to the agendas and dictates of people Min. Ben Chavis, Rev. Jesse Jackson, Rev. Al Sharpton, and hundreds of self-styled "leaders" just like them across country, is to demonstrate loyalty to King. As the last 40 years prove, this controlling device works. The ghost of King is responsible for the continued support of some of the most retrograde social policies. Most are not "leaders" at all. They wait as they observe societal trends and follow accordingly. As knee-jerk supporters of every cause espoused by the good ol boy network, they make each of these causes their own.

Although much of liberal policy has helped to undermine and destroy the last vestiges of the black family, these loyalists remain undaunted. Only now, after commentaries on recent crimes committed by blacks are publicly shaming black "leaders", have many of the notable black leaders picked up the call for blacks **"To Stop Killing Me Black Man."** Where have they been all this time that now they mention this? It will be interesting to see how many conferences, seminars and workshops can be milked out of the Bill and Melinda Gates Foundation for this latest expression of concern. The good ol boy network Need a Circle of Black leadership: Making common cause and alliances even with the morally depraved is considered "shrewd politics." NAACP function as great many black pastors fell right in line with the liberal-inspired policy of pushing condoms on children. This policy is going down to children in their early puberty years as young as 5-6th grades. Forget about whether or not parents should have a role in this, or other family member in providing this guidance, some liberals along with our "leaders" have decided that children should have these condoms. Forget about this being a parent or family responsibility, even though our tax money is being used to purchase these condoms, no one has consulted the community for its feelings on the matter especially in the black communities. To this day the rise of many so call community leaders epitomizes this tendency to mimic all things liberal. In a message of promiscuous sex to a generation of children who have already lost so much of the uniqueness of childhood, in a comical figure, never misses the opportunity to repeat favorite memorized lines: "we've taught our kids how to behave in the front seat of a car; now let's teach them how to behave in the back seat." Since civil rights game initially revolved around blacks, whites, surmised that, in order to give a particular cause the image of being part of the Universal Moral Struggle, they must enlist a circle of blacks. From abortionists to environmentalists to feminists to homosexuals, there is sure to be an auxiliary of blacks, who lend their voices to the latest homosexual-inspired crusade. It is easily understandable why homosexuals, feminists and other radical whites feel they can use the diverse population.

133

They claim their "struggles" are synonymous to black civil rights struggle, thusly they need their own Civil Rights added, to be included with black civil rights problems. When, in reality, their particular problems may have no relevance to the black struggle at all. Along with the NAACP, most black preachers (Rev. Al Sharpton who represent the Kingdom of GOD) and politicians have publicly supported the demands of homosexuals, who wish to intrude information about their debased customs into school curriculums and even to infiltrate organizations like the Boy Scouts. In contrast, the black masses have been adamant in their rejection of intrusive homosexual dogma. So much so, that Hollywood has resorted to creating a series of sentimental motion pictures, in order to put politically correct support of an AIDS-infected homosexual in the mouth of many black and white actors. We can expect so much more such propaganda devices, as blacks prove a worrisome obstacle to those promoting a sexual behavior that is clearly against the Kingdom of GODs as it is written. Our "leaders" have bought into liberal policies that have weakened laws, so that even the judicial system can no longer be counted on to protect innocent citizens from criminals and sociopaths. Worst of all, policies that have diminished the fear of strict punishment have also eliminated incentives for the young, first-time offenders to mend their ways and turn away from criminal life styles Black leaders do not hesitate to fight fellow blacks on such issues as forced school bussing. Many blacks see this as irrelevant. What we want is equal education of our children which we won't in public schools. Integration doesn't guarantee equal education even deploying legal swat teams to do so. With so many of our youth in trouble, blacks should have been among the 1st to protest removal of prayer from the schools, to further instigate sex among children. Instead, black elites were among the earliest and easiest co-opted by liberal "educators". As has long been maintained, civil rights organizations and those who earn their livings supposedly fighting for old-line civil rights causes, no longer have a place in American society. That is, their liberal views. Much of mainstream society has the same problem, but our "leaders" feel it's important for us to mimic every liberal thing mainstream society has, so why not copy them? But we can expect such people to remain intact for decades to come.

The experience of an editor who can be compared to those blacks whose lives are focused on the drives for civil rights. A former, 60s radical editor, tell of the fear that gripped him as anti-war activist, when it appeared that there might be a cessation to the Vietnam War. He says he was terrified by the thought, "What if it ends?" For his whole being was thoroughly tied to the cause of "fighting injustice" that he hardly knew where he left off and where the cause began. He claims that after the war, like many of his movement friends, he felt "cast adrift." His involvement in the anti-war movement had actually "defined" him, so who was he now? His experience can be directly applied to those blacks who possess no identity outside of The Struggle. Like the anti-war radical, if the mission were to end, where would they go to get a life? So quite naturally, all nebulous "causes" becomes fair game for "lending" black masses support. Leaders of the NAACP eagerly join many causes without even consulting the community first. They do it in their own organization, so it is quite likely the overall community has no input until it is announced. And we think everything coming out of these backroom meetings is gospel for our community because our "leaders" support it. But, unlike the anti-war radical, the civil rights activist discovered that, thru intimidation of a complaint and easily coerced American society, it could keep the "war" alive forever especially if there are many meaningless "causes" to attach themselves to. Who Loses if Blacks Win? It is in no one's interest for blacks ever to leave the sinkhole of poverty, or to form a robust, healthy business class. It's obviously not in the interest of those who are part of the immense social service industry the endless stream of social workers, counselors and growing number of "experts." It's not in the interest of civil rights organizations, whose administrators earn the finance off the needy masses. Nor is it in the interest of the black middle class whose numbers hold up the poor to demand ever more special privileges for themselves. The end of a black underclass would not be in the interests of academics, for whom the distressed poor provide material for their ever-so-clever, monographs, doctorates, journal articles, books, and inventive courses. A strong black business class certainly is not in the interest of politicians, black or white.

The black politician especially is dismayed by the prospect of a strongly developed class of entrepreneurs as potential usurpers of his power and authority. A world devoid of poor blacks is not in the interest of mainstream media, for whom our troubles provide the most for those nightly news/ entertainment shows and those grim serialized features that fill the pages of newspapers and magazines and by such many unfair stereotypes are perpetually kept in motion in the minds of all America about the black community. And, most, tragically, the loss of an underclass is not in the interest of the increasing numbers of black entertainers whose music, routines characterizations and talk shows are built around the existence of black pathologies. All it would take to begin the reversal of our community's decline are a few good men. Men determined, first, to stand against preachers, politicians and civil rights demagogues and all the bullies who are kept in place primarily through the white liberals' propaganda machine to demoralize the communities. Men ready to galvanize blacks to begin operating in best interests towards GODs Kingdom Community. Men who are ready to help return to that time in our history, when seeking the Kingdom of GOD and its Righteousness first was at the top of the agenda and all other things shall follow such as   economics, it was considered imperative to learn the workings of the marketplace, inside out. This was the legacy our ancestors had. We cannot continue down the path where our current "leaders" take advantage of our apathy for their own purposes. As economist teaches us, anybody who doesn't offer the same kind of thinking is considered such nowadays. It means that, even though the ideas may have some validity, one dares to challenge the status quo of "leadership". The "leadership" does this because it puts one on the defensive while they don't explain their ulterior motives with their Caucasian liberal friends. The community needs to know that we have to get a chance to understand which real direction we should go. Only one idea is given them, and we don't challenge our "leaders" because they are black; and they would never do anything bad for us...... NOT!

We should keep in mind the case of Singapore, which once was a subjugated colony of Great Britain. Since its liberation in 1959, Singapore's per capita income has far outstripped that of its former colonial master. The country's citizens did not look backward and whine about their   former captivity. Instead, they met the British on their own commercial turf and succeeded them. Now, in anticipation, someone may say, "but the people of Singapore did not have their culture stripped from," and more. Well, since the Harlem Renaissance and thru out our years and decades here in the US, we've developed a culture. Black Enterprise analyzed a 2012 Nielsen study that concluded that African American buying power will reach 1 Trillion dollars by 2015. So what is the excuse now? Should we be proud of just making up 13% of the total population yet spending at a rate of growth that outpaces the remaining population by 30 percent? While it is wonderful to acknowledge the report's data which shows that the Black American demographic is younger, more educated and have higher incomes than commonly believed, what can be said about the fact that we aren't retaining that wealth for the long term and at a rate sufficient to pass down wealth to subsequent generations? And it is getting worse just as this report shows we are spending more, a more recent report from the Urban Institute released in April reveals that the Black –White wealth gap has widened significantly over the past half decade It noted that in 2010, white families earned, on average, about $2 for every $1 that black families earned, a ratio that has been the same for the past 30 years. And in terms of assets, cash savings, homes and retirement accounts, subtracted from debt like mortgages and credit cards, white families have six times the wealth. And for all the spending we are doing, it's not necessarily going to help black businesses either. Although Blacks make up 13% of the US population, they own merely 5% of all US firms and only 1.8% of companies that employ more than one person, a Small Business Administration Report states. And Black owned firms are not necessarily the most profitable either. More than half of Black-owned businesses had less than $10,000 in business receipts in 2002, compared with one-third of White-owned firms and 28.8 percent of Asian-owned firms.

The report further found that on average, for every dollar that a White-owned firm made, Pacific Islander-owned firms made about 59 cents, Hispanic-, Native American-, and Asian-owned businesses made 56 cents, and Black-owned businesses made 43 cents And in this economy where sequestration is affecting contractors, it is key to note that minority firms depend more heavily on government contracting opportunities than do non minority-owned businesses, according to a 2012 report. Thus, minority-owned small businesses are suffering the most under austerity cuts. Of course, it is fair to note the role of institutions like slavery in the gap. Black workers were prevented from earning money for their labor and to build wealth to pass down. Later, institutional discrimination played a part, like that which prevented blacks from benefiting from free education via the GI Bill of the 1940s and 1950s or from the Homestead Act which awarded whites virtually free land. But since then and despite ongoing discrimination and racism as impediments, there should be an examination into whether leanings toward instant gratification purchases as opposed to saving and investing in homes, businesses and other sustainable areas are dooming our prospects to build wealth. Thus, Nielsen 1 Trillion spending and buying power by 2015 prediction is not necessarily good news when turned on its head, and juxtaposed with a not so good Black financial outlook. That report should not be a call for marketers to spend more time and energy trying to convince us to buy their stuff, but rather a call to arms to better educate ourselves on saving and growing money so that it lasts longer than one pay period. We have to move on from this point and become builders regardless. This example is very right on time if we wish to move forward. What's really killing the black community is our Godly righteous moral decline, in this regard and we need to challenge many of our so called "leaders". Such a goal was the heart of Booker T. Washington's strategy, that is, beat them at their own game. Today, he might have advised us to take our cues from the Japanese who, live by "Honor" not "Freedom" (as we do here in America) after a humiliating defeat, in WW II went on to taste the sweet revenge of economic superiority.

Even today, this country (United States of America) has much of its land and industry so intertwined with Japanese investment, so much to the point that since the 90's from the Clinton Administration to now President Obama Administration had to really watch itself in the government wishes to engage in a trade war with Japan. If the Japanese as well as China were to pull their investment capital out of the US industrial base, this country would be in serious economic trouble. When has there ever been a sweeter revenge than success? Our leadership could lead us as we press for the kinds of "rights" all Americans deserve. Right here, once our economic house is set right, and then the politicians would be beating a path to our doors for serious support. At least, we won't be taken for granted all the time, or become cannon material for more ambitious social scientists looking for a group to study. Like the right for every parent to choose his/her children's schools; the right to be free of government regulation that restricts access to the marketplace by those on the bottom rungs of the economic ladder; "The Black Man"; that's right "The Black Man" and the community. The government does this every time with its welfare programs. They stop us from using initiative and being creators of businesses, and thereby become builders. And the right to be protected from random crime, not behind the doors of our homes, but in all public places, at any time day or night. It is the black elite, as represented by the "old guard leadership", who have opened our race to meddling outsiders and mischief makers. The undermining of this leadership would strip liberals and radicals of their base of operation among blacks. Outsiders would possess no more power to control the affairs of the black community than they have among American Poles, Greeks or Asians. Heeding the call of business leaders, black men should cease reacting to circumstances created by others and begin to create new sets of conditions.

Business leaders call upon black men to "reclaim an outlook that emphasizes objectivity and personal initiative." For too long have blacks allowed whites to be the focus and reference of the black community. This attitude was reflected   recently in the comments of a prominent NY minister. Discussing some policy he was advocating, in a radio interview, he proudly stated, "We've been getting a lot of negative feedback from whites, so you know this plan must be right." Unwittingly, like so many blacks, was sending this message to our youth to measure their achievement or aims by the degree to which they can aggravate white folks. What an immature, worthless message children to be hearing from their elders. A candid exploration of the motives of certain members of the clergy is by no means to be cynical about the role of religion. Men who are genuinely committed to the Christian Gospel, and believe in its power to transform, need not feel affronted by such observations and questions. But the time as far passed for blacks to reflect on the many people who had entered the church "trade" for all the wrong reasons and, unfortunately for us, we wield a disproportionate amount of power within our community, as they continue to expand their influence by their political affiliations. In this American environment where, for decades, a clique of intellectuals have been diligently working to bring about a society   emptied of conventional values personal religious faith is more critical than ever. As mainstream society veers away from the security of traditional religious anchors and nurtures, forces determined to destroy long-cherished supports, blacks are greatly affected. If mainstream society is going down the tubes morally, it appears our "leaders" who so much may still cling to the last trace of integration, want our community to go down those same tubes. The black community is a part of GODs Kingdom Community and as we have our own destiny forged by our fore fathers, we also need to get back to "Our Father, The Almighty GOD".

Using the moral force derived from religion, whether it is rooted in Christianity or Islam the two religious cultures to which most blacks adhere, black men should take the lead in opposing those who are working to abolish every trace of Christianity in American life. As black men, we are not speaking up and taking the offensive on the righteous moral high ground in the black community. Consequently black families, from this moral standpoint, are falling apart from within. And no political movements can restore the damage of the black families turning away from righteous spiritual and moral heritage. As Citizens of the Kingdom of GOD the   Christian black family must reject those who, is assisted by an all powerful media, are vengefully going about the task of diluting the Word of GOD, while replacing them with trendy psychotherapeutic fetishes, twelve Step programs and "self help" 800 numbers. As crime and broken families unravel American society at the seams, the black family should join with righteous activists Christians, religious Jews, and Muslims believers, to root back the poisonous tide that is eroding our righteous moral climate. Booker T. Washington was not the first to acknowledge the link between the economic and the spiritual need. He repeatedly emphasized how closely the "moral and spiritual interests" are interwoven with a group's material and economic wealth." And it should also be noted that Booker T. Washington wasn't the first to understand this. In the Book of Proverbs: 14:34, it says, "righteousness exalts a nation, but sin is a reproach to any people." Strengthening our resolve to ground our   families in righteous moral values will better prepare us to compete on all fronts, including the economic one. So we have to ask ourselves, now that we understand how we drifted so far off course as a people, we need to pray to God to help us get back to Him and stay connected. They don't understand righteous moral issues such as the decline of our families, that can't be solved via political fronts. The black family needs a spiritual   rejuvenation. Some "preachers" are trying to do this and they should push for GREATER GODLY PRINCIPLES. Other Preachers should know better, by trying to solve problems which have been rooted via political fronts. And we have to challenge our "leaders" when they hand us "traditional solutions via government programs instead of "The Kingdom of GODs" government program.

CHAPTER VIII

Abomination

Of

Desolation

"So when you see standing in the Holy place 'the abomination that causes desolation,' spoken of through the prophet Daniel—let the reader understand— then let those who are in Judea flee to the mountains. Let no one on the housetop go down to take anything out of the house. Let no one in the field go back to get their cloak. How dreadful it will be in those days for pregnant women and nursing mothers! Pray that your flight will not take place in winter or on the Sabbath. For then there will be great distress, unequaled from the beginning of the world until now— and never to be equaled again. "If those days had not been cut short, no one would survive, but for the sake of the elect those days will be shortened. Matt 24:15-22. The setting up of the "abomination of desolation" is the one most important event signaling the beginning of the Great Tribulation! But what is it? Where is it to be set up? Who, or what, does it represent? When will we see it in place? Matthew warned, "Whoso read, let him understand," so God intends we should understand what Christ meant not be ignorant of one of the most important events in future history. Christ's warning about an "abomination of desolation" means, literally, "the abomination of the desolater," which all authorities generally agree meant an idol, or idolatrous apparatus, to be set up in the holy place by the individual who would destroy Jerusalem, or cause it to become "desolate."

An "abomination" is something God detests, and comes from the Hebrew word shakaz, for an idol; something, or someone who is worshiped in place of the true God. Christ specifically stated He was referring to the same thing written in the book of Daniel. Daniel's prophecy mentions this "abomination" several times: Daniel 9:27; 11:31 and 12:2 are examples. These scriptures identify, in symbol, the perpetrator of Daniel's prophecy. Some say "This appears to have been a prediction of the pollution of the temple by Antiochus Epiphanes, who caused an idolatrous altar to be built on the altar of burnt offerings, whereon unclean things were offered to Jupiter Olympius, to whom the temple itself was dedicated" Daniel wrote of a "little horn" coming up among the ten horns of the beast a symbol of a government, or ruler, who succeeds in overthrowing three successive kings, then holds sway over the final seven heads of the holy Roman Empire. Of the abomination of desolation and the one who puts it in place, Daniel wrote, "Yea, he magnified himself even to the prince of the host, and by him the daily sacrifice was taken away, and the place of the sanctuary was cast down" (Daniel 8:11). Historian Theologians says, "Though robbed of its treasures, it was not strictly 'cast down' by Antiochus; so that a fuller accomplishment is future. Antiochus took away the daily sacrifice for a few years; the Romans, for many ages, and 'cast down' the temple; and Antichrist, in connection with Rome, the fourth kingdom, shall do so again, after the Jews in their own land, still unbelieving, shall have rebuilt the temple and   restored the Mosaic ritual". Obviously, since Antiochus reigned hundreds of years before Christ, his desecration of the temple was only a forerunner of Daniel's prophecy, which is referring to the time of the end (Daniel 12:4-11). A second forerunner of this prophesied event took place shortly after Christ's warning prophecy of Matthew 24:15, at the destruction of Jerusalem by the armies of Titus. "This may with probability be referred to the advance of the Roman army against the city with their image-crowned standards, to which idolatrous honors were paid, and which the Jews regarded as idols. The unexpected retreat and discomfiture of the Roman forces afforded such as were mindful of our Saviors prophecy an opportunity of obeying the injunction which it   contained, (Christ's warning Mat. 24:16 that they should 'flee to the mountains.')".

There was another later and more specific abomination of the holy place accomplished by emperor Hadrian, who with "...studied insult to the Jews, set up the figure of a boar over the Bethlehem gate of the city which rose upon the site and ruins of Jerusalem, but he erected a temple to Jupiter upon the site of the Jewish temple and caused an image of himself to be set up in the part which answered to the most holy place. These abominations, which took place over a vast span of time in history, are not the fulfillment of Christ's end-time prophecy! Notice again the time setting of Christ's Olivet prophecy: "When you therefore shall see the abomination of desolation...stand in the holy place...then let them which be in Jerusalem flee into the mountains...for then shall be a GREAT TRIBULATION such as was not since the beginning of the world to this time, no, nor ever shall be. "And except those days should be shortened, there should no flesh be saved, but for the elect's sake, those days shall be shortened" (Matthew 24:15-22). The warning concerning the final abomination to be set up in the "holy place" is directly connected to the beginning of the great tribulation, which has as one of its main features the horrible martyrdom of saints (Daniel 7:20-21; Matthew 24:9). Notice! "All these are the beginning of sorrows of the tribulation." Christ said the tribulation would be a time unparalleled in all history. Notice what Daniel wrote: "At that time Michael, the great prince who protects your people, will arise. There will be a time of distress such as has not happened from the beginning of nations until then. But at that time your people—everyone whose name is found written in the book—will be delivered. (Daniel 12:1). There cannot be two such times, for each is the superlative the worst time of "trouble," meaning droughts, famines, disease epidemics, the unleashing of horrifying, death-dealing weapons of destruction in war that has ever taken place since civilization began! But wait. Daniel said, "And at that time..." (Daniel 12:1). At what time? The chapter break interrupts a flow of thought from Daniel 11:40 to 45. The "king of the south" was, anciently, one of the Ptolemys of Egypt, a lesser dynasty of pharaohs who waged war with Syria. Syria and Egypt were but two of the four smaller kingdoms left after Alexander's death (Daniel 11:4). The "king of the north" was, eventually, the same Antiochus Epiphanes who set up a typical abomination of desolation.

But the prophecy is specifically stated to be for a definite time in history "the TIME OF THE END" (Daniel 11:40). Therefore, Ptolemy Soter and Antiochus Epiphanes are but types, historical representatives, of the two human leaders who will be used to fulfill this end-time prophecy. Probably, the man who will fulfill the role of "king of the south" will be an Arab leader. He will "push at" the "king of the north," who is the same personage as the beast of Bible prophecy. The expression "push at," seems to fall short of armed aggression. Is it some political affront? Could it have been an oil embargo, or threatened disruption of energy to Europe and the world? Because of Saddam Hussein's occupation of Kuwait, and the result concentration of military forces and supplies from about thirty nations in the Persian Gulf region, many are tempted to assign Saddam the role of one of the two, either the "king of the north," or the "king of the south." Certainly, Saddam Hussein was "pushing at" others. But was he "pushing at" someone called "the king of the north," or any modern day political/military leader who is filling such a role? No, Hussein was "pushing at" the United States, Britain, France, Germany, the Soviet Union, Israel, Japan, and Saudi Arabia indeed, the nations of the world! The response to Saddam Hussein was not a sudden occupation of Israel, Egypt, and other nearby countries by some northern power, but the deployment of hundreds of thousands of troops into Saudi Arabia. Notice that the reaction of the "king of the north" is not protracted economic embargo, or warfare in the Persian Gulf, but a lightning-like attack into Israel, and "many countries" in the region, including Egypt! (Daniel 11:40-42). It is not Europe, or the United States threatening to invade Israel in this past crisis but Saddam Hussein of Iraq. Daniel 11:40-45 do not leap to impossible conclusions, nor should it lead one to become hysterical about the nearness of "Armageddon." Israel and Egypt are both occupied by this "king of the north" at the end time. Daniel 11:40-45 absolutely precludes the possibility that the "king of the north" could be an Islamic leader, for Egypt is an Islamic nation, the largest in population of all Islam. Egypt is Arabic, and, though currently observing the Camp David accords, is nevertheless staunchly united religiously and emotionally with all other Arab nations in calling for the withdrawal of Israel from the "occupied territory of GAZA." No other Arab state would occupy Egypt.

This is the final head of the "holy Roman Empire" which was always a Germanic power! The king of the north is the final beast of prophecy. Now, when does this northern military power come storming into Israel? "At the time of the end," says Daniel. And then Daniel 12:1, we see Daniel's prophecy that at that time" Michael stands up, and a time of trouble such as never was since there was a nation begins! In other words, the great tribulation. So the tribulation commences at the same time this king of the north invades. Christ's warning about the abomination of desolation included this invasion of nations by armies. Those forces are identified in Daniel 11:40-45 as being the forces of the king of the north. Christ said, "When you see Jerusalem being surrounded by armies, you will know that its desolation is near. (Luke 21:20). Christ warned, "Then when the abomination of desolation is set up let them which are in Judaea flees into the mountains..." He continues to say the flight is so urgent; so sudden, that one should not return to retrieve clothing, or household items even food! He warned, "Let him which is on the housetop not come down to take anything out of his house: "Neither let him which is in the field return back to take his clothes" (Matthew 24:16-18).Those to whom this warning applies will not read of some impending attack in their weekly news magazines, or see it on nightly television for months at a time it will occur SUDDENLY, with shocking swiftness. The scene set by Christ is of a normal working day where a man might be in the fields, his wife on top of the roof, hanging up washing. Yet, suddenly, when people least expect it, attacking military forces are seen around Jerusalem. In the Jerusalem of Christ's day, houses were set adjoining each other. Roofs were flat, with parapets, and were used for sitting and talking, hanging up washing, play areas for children, even sleeping at night in hot weather. Commonly, families would erect temporary shelters of fronds and branches, and move into these little booths during the Feast of Tabernacles. The rabbis wrote of the "road of the roofs," wherein one might walk across several adjoining rooftops, then descend to the street without having to go back inside one's own house. Christ referred to this practice in His warning. Daniel's prophecy says the tribulation is the time when Michael stands up.

Michael is identified as "Michael your prince" (Daniel 10:20-21) an archangel who is the prince of Israel. Daniel 12: says Michael is to stand "for the children of Israel," the children of the people of Daniel, who was a noble of Israel. Christ's prophecy specifically pointed out events to take place in Jerusalem; the Middle East, and Palestine! But the Great Tribulation will be global in its effects, for Christ said, as did Daniel, that it will be a "time of trouble such as there has not been from the time there was a nation"! He also said that if God did not cut short this terrible time of global trouble, not a man, woman, or child would be left alive (Matthew 24:21-22). Therefore, while events in Jerusalem provide a positive sign that the tribulation is beginning, the tribulation is not confined to Palestine, and the city of Jerusalem. Yet, from Christ's warnings, we see it is obvious the great tribulation begins in Jerusalem; in Palestine, by the setting up of an "abomination," which causes desolation, or destruction. Specifically, the abomination is to be set up in the temple, but no temple exists as yet. The terrible loss of life depicted by Christ is to begin in Jerusalem and neighboring areas the modern nation called "Israel." Christ's stern warning, together with Daniel's prophecies, show Jerusalem occupied by a northern military power. But the Jews in "Israel" are but one tribe, with perhaps increments of two others Judah, together with some of Levi and Simeon. There were thirteen tribes in all, counting the two half-tribes of Joseph, Ephraim and Manasseh. The northern ten tribes, with a separate dynasty of kings commencing from the time of Jeroboam, and a separate national capitol, were carried away captive by Assyrian kings long prior to the captivity of Judah. The ten tribes disappeared into the bleak steppes between the Black and Caspean seas during the years 721 to 718 BC! It was not until 540 BC, about 178 years later, that Judah was taken captive into Babylon. The bulk of those deported Israelites never returned to Palestine. They migrated along the river valleys into Europe, and into the British Isles! Jacob, the grandson of Abraham, was renamed "Israel" after his tenacious encounter with God. Jacob had twelve sons, each of whom became the eponymous ancestor of a large tribe of people. Jacob was called "Israel" from the time of his renaming.

Judah, one of his sons, together with major portions of Simeon and Levi, came to be known as the "House of Judah," while Manasseh, Ephraim, Gad, Asher, Dan, Naphtali, Benjamin, Reuben, Issachar and Zebulun became known as the "House of Israel" The two are never synonymous in the Bible. There are four books of the Bible detailing the separate national histories of these two distinctly different nations; different dynasties of kings, different territories, different national capitols different languages, cultures, and religions! The very first time the "nickname" for Judah, "Jew," is ever used in the Bible, the Jews are at war against Israel! Now, notice that the Great Tribulation comes not only upon the Jews in the modern nation called Israel, but upon the "House of Jacob," or "The House of Israel," as well! "Alas! for that day is great, so that none is like it an unparalleled time exactly as described in Matthew 24:15 and Daniel 12:1 the same time of the Great Tribulation: it is even the time of Jacob's trouble; but he shall be saved out of it" (Jeremiah 30:7). What is the Great Tribulation? It is a time of horrible suffering; disease, famine, starvation, and the grisly death of millions as a result of terrible warfare featuring the ghastly weapons of modern technology which is to come on the United States, Britain, Canada, Australia, South Africa, and several of the democracies of northwestern Europe. It will especially impact the modern nation called "Israel," the Jews in Palestine! Christ's somber Olivet Prophecy again. He said, referring to the temple and its great buildings and walls, "..."Do you see all these things?" he asked. "Truly I tell you, not one stone here will be left on another; everyone will be thrown down." (Matthew 24:2). Later, He said, "And this gospel of the Kingdom shall be preached in all the world for a witness a witness AGAINST them unto all nations and THEN shall the end come" (Matthew 24:14). The Gospel was not preached to but a few prior to Christ's death. He spoke in puzzling parables to the masses (Matthew 13:10-17), explaining to His disciples that it was not yet given to them to understand. It was not until after His resurrection, and His appearance to His disciples (Acts. 1:7-8) that He told them to spread out from Palestine, to the "uttermost parts of the earth," preaching the Gospel. By 70 AD, only a comparative few had heard the Gospel of the Kingdom of God.

It had by no means been preached as a witness to the world. Yet, Christ gave this as a major prerequisite to the setting up of the abomination of desolation. God will not leave this world without a witness. God will not allow anyone to plaintively cry, "But you never told me!" Just as He sent several of His prophets to loudly proclaim the impending national punishments coming upon the ten-tribe of Israel long before their destruction detailing their horrible sins; their stiff-necked, God-defying rebellion; their Sabbath-breaking and consequent idolatry; just as He sent several of His prophets to warn Judah of its impending destruction by the Babylonian armies; just as Christ warned His generation (Matthew 24) of the impending destruction of Jerusalem by Titus, SO GOD IS SENDING HIS WARNING AND WITNESS TO THIS WORLD, TODAY! Most so-called evangelists respond to the cry from people, "preach smooth things; speak deceits!" (Isaiah 30:10). Where, on weekly television, in the thousands of pulpits across our lands, or in religious literature, do you find those who are solemnly telling their audiences that our nations are going to be brutally CONQUERED IN GLOBAL WARFARE unless we repent of our personal and collective sins? Christ warned, "...except ye repent, ye shall all likewise perish" (Luke 13:3, 5). When the armies of Titus destroyed the city of Jerusalem, tens of thousands of Jews were slaughtered. Yet, countless ones among them had heard Christ's warning, and the warnings of His faithful apostles and ministers in the years that followed! Instead of repenting, they rejected Christ, and soon began killing and throwing into jail His apostles! Except for a few Jews who fled to Pella after the high priest allegedly heard an audible voice in the temple, telling him to flee (according to Josephus), and the bulk of the population experienced a holocaust! Christ's stern warning had come true! The soldiers prized loose even the stones atop the walls of the temple. The temple was eventually destroyed. But Christ specifically stated that, immediately following the Great Tribulation, there would come spectacular heavenly signs. "Immediately after the tribulation of those days shall the sun be darkened, and the moon shall not give her light, and the stars meteorites shall fall from heaven and the powers of the heaven shall be shaken:

And then shall appear the sign of the Son of Man in heaven: and then shall the tribes of the earth mourn, and they shall see the Son of man coming in the clouds of heaven with power and great glory" (Matthew 24:27-30). Therefore, the prophecy in Matthew 24, Mark 13 and Luke 21 is dual; it has a typical, early fulfillment, and a literal, final end-time fulfillment! Jerusalem is destined to be destroyed again unless its inhabitants repent. There were no heavenly signs at the destruction of Jerusalem by the armies of Titus; Christ did not come in the power of the Almighty God, shaking the heavens, causing the sun to become black as sackcloth of ashes! Therefore, there is coming, yet, another destruction of Jerusalem! It will be signaled by the emplacement of the abomination that makes desolate. Now, who is to set up this abomination? The four great, successive world-dominating empires of Babylon, Persia, Greco/Macedonia and Rome are depicted in both Daniel 2 and Daniel 7. At the conclusion of the description of the final one of these kingdoms, ROME, Daniel says, "But the saints of the Most High shall take the kingdom, and possess the kingdom forever, even forever and ever" (Daniel 7:18). Daniel then said, "Then I would know the truth of the fourth beast (Rome), which was diverse from all the others, exceeding dreadful, whose teeth were of iron, and his nails of brass; which devoured, brake in pieces, and stamped the residue with his feet; "And of the ten horns that were in his head, and of the other (a separate, different "horn," or government; a ruler) which came up, and before whom three fell" (Daniel 7:19-20). This prophecy shows the ten "horns," or governments, were successive, and not contemporaneous. That this "little horn" is not one of the successive ten is equally obvious, for it is "another" horn which was seen to arise. Notice its description, "I considered the horns (ten of them), and, behold, there came up among them another little horn, before whom there were three of the first horns (these probably were the Vandals, Ostragoths, and the Heruli) plucked up by the roots: and, behold, in this horn were eyes like the eyes of man, and a mouth speaking great things."

I beheld till the thrones were cast down, and the Ancient of days did sit, whose garment was white as snow...a fiery stream issued and came forth from before Him: thousand thousands ministered unto Him, and ten thousand times ten thousand stood before Him: the judgment was set, and the books were opened" (Daniel 7:8-10). This is obvious reference to the Second Coming of Christ, the beginning of His millennial reign, and the final judgment day! Yet, the prophecy commences with the emergence of the "little horn;" separate from the other ten; distinctly different, who succeeds in overthrowing, or uprooting, the first three "horns" or governments, of the fourth beast of Daniel 7. The "Antichrist rises after their rise, at first 'little,' (v. 8) but after destroying three of the ten he becomes greater than them all (vv. 20, 21). The three being gone, he is the eighth; a distinct head, and yet 'of the seven'. Now, what of the "mouth speaking great things"? Daniel says, "And of the ten horns that were in his head, and of the other which came up the "little horn", and before whom three the first three, in succession fell; even that horn that had eyes of a man, and a mouth that spoke great things, whose look was more stout than his fellows."I beheld, and the same horn made war with the saints, and   prevailed against them!" (Daniel 7:20-21). So much for the idea of "raptured" saints who are not on earth at the time of the tribulation, or special "saints" who is hiding out in caves. Notice that this applies literally to the final two witnesses, who are killed by the Antichrist power (Revelation 11:7), and also applies to the church (Revelation 13:7). This "little horn" represents some kind of government which persecutes God's true church! Four separate times in Daniel's seventh chapter, the prophecy commences with visions of the fourth beast (Rome), being   controlled by a "little horn" which overthrows the first three successive governments of Rome, but which is still extant at the time of the end, persecuting the true church, to be finally destroyed by Christ Himself, at His Second Coming. In other words, the Bible "dates" the time of the "little horn," identifying it as a power, or government, which will be actively persecuting God's people at the time of Christ's return! Now, who does this persecuting what power, or government, is responsible for the martyrdom of God's true servants? "And he this same "little horn" shall speak great words against the most High, and shall wear out the saints of the most High, and think to change times and laws: and they the saints shall be given into his hand until a time one year and times two more years and the dividing of time six months, or one half year; three and one half years in all.

"But the judgment shall sit, and they shall take away his dominion, to consume and to destroy it unto the end" (Daniel 7:25-26). This shows a period of terrible persecutions and martyrdom of three and one-half years! And it is at the time of the end, from the beginning of the tribulation until the Second Coming of Christ! This "little horn" symbolizes a human leader who sits in a position powerful enough to assay to change times and laws Daniel heard one angel ask another, "How long shall the vision concerning the daily sacrifice, and the transgression of desolation the abomination of desolation, to give both the sanctuary and the host to be trodden under foot?"And he said unto me, Unto two thousand and three hundred days; then shall the sanctuary be cleansed" (Daniel 8:13-14). So the abomination of desolation will be set in place, defiling the sanctuary, for three and one-half years! John wrote, "And they worshipped the dragon (Satan) which gave power unto the beast: and they worshipped the beast (extreme nationalism state worship!), saying, 'Who is able to make war with him?' "And there was given unto him a mouth speaking great things and blasphemies (the same mouth as that of the "little horn," meaning Antichrist; the great false prophet!); and power was given unto him to continue forty and two months" (Revelation 13:4-5). When the Antichrist establishes himself, setting up the abomination, he will continue for three and one-half years. Notice further: "And there was given me a reed likes unto a rod: and the angel stood, saying, Rise, and measure the temple of God, and the altar, and them that worship therein."But the court which is without the temple leave out, and measures it not, for it is given unto the Gentiles: and the holy city shall they tread under foot forty and two months" Revelation 11:1-2). During this three-and-one-half year period, all organized preaching of the Gospel is impossible. God's church is scattered, persecuted. (Amos 8:11). Some are to be martyred many are to be miraculously protected from the Antichrist. God says, "And when the dragon saw that he was cast unto the earth, he persecuted the woman which brought forth the man child (the church), "And to the woman were given two wings of a great eagle (symbolic of God's miraculous protection. Exodus 19:4) that she might fly into the wilderness, into her place, where she is nourished for a time, and times, and half a time (three and one-half years!) from the face of the serpent. "And the serpent cast out of his mouth water as a flood after the woman, that he might cause her to be carried away of the flood."And the earth helped the woman, and the earth opened her mouth, and swallowed up the flood which the dragon cast out of his mouth.

"And the dragon was wroth with the woman, and went to make war with the remnant of her seed, which keep the commandments of God, and have the testimony of Jesus Christ" (Revelation 12:13-17). Some have seen the "flood" in historical terms; the entire period of the dominance of the "little horn" over the heads of the Holy Roman Empire, and the "flood" of lying doctrines, false charges, and propaganda spewed out of the mouth of the woman who rides the beast. Some have thought it to be literal; a miracle brought about by Satan, from which God's people are delivered, like a type of the Red Sea. Whatever its meaning, Satan fails in his attempt to destroy God's church. Nevertheless, God's Word says the great false church, led by its "man of sin" who is Antichrist, will horribly persecute God's saints. The Great Tribulation includes the martyrdom of many of God's servants (Matthew 24:9; Revelation 13:7). Not all of God's people will be protected. For example, the two witnesses, two human beings who will be specially anointed to be God's last two prophets warning the beast and false prophet, are to be killed by the Antichrist and the beast. The work of the two witnesses takes place at the exact same period during which the abomination of desolation sits; the time of the "treading down of the sanctuary." "And I will give power unto my two witnesses, and they shall prophesy a thousand, two hundred and threescore days, clothed in sackcloth...these have power to shut heaven, that it rain not in the days of their prophecy: and have power over waters to turn them to blood, and to smite the earth with all plagues, as often as they will."And when they shall have finished their testimony, the beast that ascendeth out of the bottomless pit shall make war against them, and shall overcome them, and kill them" (Revelation 11:3-7). Some have assumed the whole church will be "taken to a place of safety" for the three and one-half years. Obviously not. Are not these two witnesses' members of God's true church? Are they not converted, with God's Holy Spirit, and therefore members of the spiritual "body of Christ," which is the church? Yet, God allows their martyrdom. Even as God sent the plagues on Egypt while Israel was yet in the land of Goshen, making a "difference" between the Israelites and Egyptians; even as the death angel "passed over" the Israelites houses and killed the firstborn of Egypt; so God promises, "A thousand shall fall at thy side, and ten thousand at thy right hand, but it shall not come nigh thee (Psalm 91:1-9). God's captive people Israel are pictured as crying out to Him in the time of their horrible tribulation:

153

This is a great mother church, which has daughters which came out of her in protest! She wears the colors of whoredom, uses names and titles which are blasphemous, and teaches doctrines cloaked in mystery. She holds the same old "mystery religion" that dates to ancient Babylon; to the time of Semiramis and Nimrod, the founders of the Babylon mystery religion, and of organized cities and governments of man. Her main trappings are the sun; bowing toward the rising sun in the east on the ancient day dedicated to "Ishtar" (Semiramis), pronounced "Easter," today; worship on Sunday instead of God's Holy Sabbath; sanctioning the use of purely pagan symbols of sexual reproduction and offspring like orbs and bulbs, the "Ishtar" lily, phallic symbols, flies, eggs a seemingly endless array of the accouterments of ancient heathenism. She has always fought God's truth, and persecuted God's converted servants. Countless thousands have been put to death for daring to cling to the Sabbath; to God's sacred Passover, which was always held on the evening of the 14th of Nisan by Christ and His disciples. Notice more of this woman's description: And I saw the woman drunken with the blood of the saints, and with the blood of the martyrs of Jesus: and when I saw her, I wondered with great admiration (astonishment, not approbation) (Revelation 17:5-6). She is instrumental in binding together the final ten nations comprising the beast. It is her influence and doctrine which provides the "clay" for the ten toes of Daniel's second chapter; a weak bonding agent which is not mixed with the "iron" of the militarily powerful nation which will dominate the ten. Now, notice how this great false church is the same entity as the second beast of Revelation 13! "And I beheld another beast coming up out of the earth; and he had two horns like a lamb (it appears Christ-like), and he spoke as a dragon (as Satan: Revelation 12:9)."And he exercised all the power of the first beast before him, the first beast of Revelation 13 is the same beast as the fourth beast of Daniel 7; representing Imperial Rome from the time of the earliest Roman emperors, and Romulus who gave Rome its name, to the latter-day rulers of the "holy Roman Empire" and caused the earth and them that dwell therein to worship the first beast, whose deadly wound was healed" (Revelation 13:11-12). This deadly wound was the fall of Imperial Rome in 476. Its healing was in 554, when Belesarius, victorious in northern Africa, was instrumental in restoring the power of Rome.

Notice that this false religious leader, the "little horn" who thought to change times and laws, who was full of names of blasphemy, and who martyred God's saints is empowered by Satan to perform miracles. "And he does great wonders, so that he makes fire come down from heaven on the earth in the sight of men, and deceives them that dwell on the earth by the means of those miracles which he had power to do in the sight of the beast; saying to them that dwell on the earth, that they should make an image of the beast, that the image of the beast should both speak (he has a "mouth speaking great things") and cause that as many as would not worship the image of the beast should be killed" (Revelation 13:11-15).Where do you find a great, global church whose leader claims infallibility; the authority to change "times and laws," to establish dogma? Where is the great, multi-lingual, multi-national, universal church which conducts its religious ceremonies in mysteries, in mysterious symbolism, in elaborate rituals with various hidden meanings? Where is there a great church which is a powerful political organization, having vast influence over geopolitics; over political decisions like choice of government for masses of peoples in many different nations? Where is the great church whose leaders dress in red and scarlet, the colors of harlotry? Where is the great church which boasts it is "eternal"? Which city is the "eternal" city, according to lore; the city of "seven hills"? John's vision continued, "The seven heads are seven mountains on which the woman sits" (Revelation 17:9). He went on to say, The woman you saw is the great city that rules over the kings of the earth." (Revelation 17:18). Which city can claim to have ruled over "the kings of the earth" down through history? Certainly not Washington, D.C., or London, or Berlin, or Tokyo, or Moscow. Which, then? Where is a church whose leader is courted by the most powerful political leaders in the world a church leader who has the power to incite massive demonstrations, strikes, rebellions which can unseat political systems and bring about revolutions in government? This same great false church is mentioned by Isaiah. Notice, you said, 'I am forever—the eternal queen!' But you did not consider these things or reflect on what might happen. "Now then, listen, you lover of pleasure, lounging in your security and saying to yourself, 'I am, and there is none besides me. I will never be a widow or suffer the loss of children.'(Isaiah 47:7-8). Which great church is called "mother" by all others?

Which church has protesting daughters which came out of her, and which she confidently boasts she will bring back to the fold? (But her daughters will share her fate: Isaiah 47:9). John's prophecy shows how this great church uses the power of the state to carry out her wishes: "And he had power to give life unto the image of the beast, that the image of the beast should both speak, and cause as many as would not worship the image of the beast should be killed. "And he causes all, both small and great, rich and poor, free and bond, to receive a mark in their right hand (symbolizing cooperation, agreement, willingness, commitment to work), or in their foreheads (symbolizing like-mindedness, cooperation, acceptance, agreement): and that no man might buy or sell, save he had the mark, or the name of the beast, or the number of his name. "Here is wisdom. Let him that has understanding count the number of the beast: for it is the number of a man: and his number is Six hundred threescore and six" (Revelation 13:15-18). The beast is Rome, from the time of Imperial Rome to the present to the end-time resurrection of the same old system in the heartland of Europe, dominated by one great religion, which will hold sway over all ten nations. The "image" is the church which was designed and constructed along the same lines as Imperial Rome, with the diocese, the great diocese, a "collegia," or "college of cardinals," and an absolute ruler, claiming the "primacy of Peter" whose word is unquestioned! The "image" of the beast is its length and shadow, its replica, its copy. Yet, it is a religious organization, having the appearance of a lamb, but speaking like a dragon, like Satan! To obey it is to receive its identifying signs and symbols, or its mark. The image of the beast is, therefore, a great false church organization, patterned after the political structure of ancient, Imperial Rome, with a human leader so revered that many attribute to him virtual divinity (Roman emperors claimed to be god; to be divine, in some instances); a church organization which cloaks many of its rituals and beliefs in mysteries, and a church organization having political influence concourse with governments of the world a church which is at once a state, having full political sovereignty like that of any other nation. Now you can understand the vision of the ten-horned beast (the final resurrection of the same old system called the "Holy Roman Empire") being ridden by the great fallen woman.

From the very beginning of the New Testament church which Christ founded (Matthew 16:18), elements from both within and without (Acts 20:28-31) sought to rid God's true church of everything remotely "Jewish." This came about as a result of massive numbers of Gentiles joyously embracing Christianity many of them wanting to cling to ancient, pagan traditions. The New Testament, particularly Paul's writings and the "letters to the churches" in Revelation 2 and 3, is a story of the erosion of the original faith; of attacks from Judaism, who could not seem to shake the concept of circumcision, and who wished to impose the principles of Judaism, not Christianity, on new converts (1 Corinthians 7:18-19). Continually, the fledgling New Testament church is seen struggling against persecutions from government; from the leaders of the Jewish religious sects; from apostasies within and from attacks without. Paul's letter to the Galatians marvels at how soon they had listened to "another Gospel," and heard about "another Jesus" (Galatians 1:6-8). He rebukes the Corinthians, who, reverting to their pagan customs, had turned the Passover into a Bacchian night of revelry; who tolerated incest within their ranks. He continually defends himself against "false apostles" who parade their "Jewishness" to the people (2 Corinthians 11-12). Jude, the next to the last book of the New Testament, appeals to true Christians to get back to the "faith once delivered," showing how far the apostasy had progressed. Jude is a clear warning against false teachers who reverted to the pagan mysteries; used gluttony, revelry, sexual promiscuity in their religious services, exactly as heathen priestesses functioned as "temple prostitutes," claiming that such activities were symbolic of concourse with the deity. By the time John wrote the book of Revelation, probably about 91 or 92 AD, the apostasy was nearly complete. In the second and third chapters, in the letters to the churches, you will see the churches plagued with false doctrines, false religious leaders, false practices a church shot through with paganism! Acts 8 and other scriptures identify a man who may have risen to become the first major leader of this apostasy; a man who may well have masqueraded as the "Peter" of Rome, Simon the Magus, or Simon the Magician. His story would require book-length investigation. However, he passed into history, and is not relevant today, except as a forerunner of the final false prophet.

However, he passed into history, and is not relevant today, except as a forerunner of the final false prophet. Paul wrote of the budding apostasy, and made it clear that a false Prophet will rise in the last days just prior to the Second Coming of Christ! "Let no man deceive you by any means: for that day shall not come (the Second Coming of Christ), except there come a falling away (apostasy!) first, and that man of sin be revealed, the son of perdition; "Who opposes and exalts himself above all that is called God, or that is worshipped; so that he as God sits in the temple of God (a temple which is yet to be constructed in Jerusalem!), showing himself (claiming) that he is God. "...And now ye know what withholds [withstands; resists. Paul is speaking of himself, as one who was "holding back" this growing apostasy] that he might be revealed in his time. "For the mystery of iniquity [it was a "mystery" religion; one which condoned sin, or "iniquity"] doth already work; only he who now let's [restrains] will let [continue to restrain], until he be taken out of the way" (2 Thessalonians 2:1-7). Here we see a human religious leader who will ensconce himself inside the temple in Jerusalem and actually claim to be divine! Claim to be God! The expression, "be taken out of the way" is the subject of some contention. The Greek verb is ginomai, which carries the connotation "become to be." The preferred reading may well be, "until he 'become to be,'" or "become evident for who he is," rather than a reference to Paul, as one who would be removed by death, or "taken out of the way." Either way, the meaning is clear that Paul was one of the last restraining influences against virtual total apostasy in the early church; that following his death there would be no one left in the eastern world who withstood it. Yet, Paul's writing was also prophetic, for he referred to the end time, and not just the few years following his death. Gradually, the visible church of the first and second centuries dramatically changed. Little by little purely pagan customs were adopted. Pagans coming into the church carried with them their superstitions, their various holidays and observances. Liberal clergymen, ever desirous of more money and power, of larger followings, permitted these pagan customs, dressing them up in "Christian" trappings. Some of these power-hungry leaders gained control of the physical properties of the church through exercising autocratic authority over the people. John wrote of one "Diotrephes," who coveted power, and who "put out" from that local congregation the true believers, retaining only those who had prostituted themselves, spiritually, to corrupt human power (3 John). Easter finally replaced the Passover. Sunday replaced the Sabbath.

To be the sole human leader under Christ! This is one Christmas obscured the time of Christ's conception. By the time of the Council of Nicaea in 325 AD, true Christians were solemnly warned against "Judaism" by continuing to obey God in observing His Sabbaths, or following Christ's example of observing the Passover on the 14th of Nisan; instead, they were commanded to observe the purely pagan "Ishtar" festival, in honor of the pagan goddess of fecundity and sex; a springtime celebration featuring rapidly-reproducing rabbits, the symbols of eggs, and other "mystical" paraphernalia. From that time to this, the professing "Christian" world has followed the great apostate church. Millions observe "Ishtar" (pronounced "Easter," today) with bunnies and eggs; facing the rising sun in the east, and eating "hot cross buns" (from bous, or boun, meaning the symbol of Taurus, the bull Tammuz, or Nimrod), and reveling in a pagan celebration which has been dressed up in "Christian" clothing. Eventually, the millions of adherents to this pagan "mystery" religion, now masquerading as "Christian," would bring about the requirement for kings and emperors to acknowledge the power of the church, or suffer the consequences the sure loss of ruler ship, and perhaps the loss of their lives! God solemnly warned His people never to be part of this Babylon mystery religion; not to partake of its intrigues, its political goals, its wars, or its political systems. "And I heard another voice from heaven, saying, 'COME OUT OF HER, MY PEOPLE, that ye be not partakers of her sins, and that ye receive not of her plagues,' For her sins have reached unto heaven, and God hath remembered her iniquities" (Revelation 18:4-5). The 18th chapter of Revelation details how the ten-nation beast power shall finally "hate the whore," and utterly destroys this false church, putting to death countless thousands of its officials and its peoples. God will finally reward this hideous, waddling old madam of religion, this persecutor and torturer of God's people, with the bitterest dregs of the cup of wrath! That is why God warns His people to forsake this mystery religion that they "receive not of her plagues. Christ had instructed His disciples, "If the world hates you, keep in mind that it hated me first. If you belonged to the world, it would love you as its own. As it is, you do not belong to the world, but I have chosen you out of the world. That is why the world hates you. (John 15:18-19).

He continued, in His prayer to the Father just before His death and resurrection, I have given them your word and the world has hated them, for they are not of the world any more than I am of the world. My prayer is not that you take them out of the world but that you protect them from the evil one. They are not of the world, even as I am not of it. Sanctify them by the truth; your word is truth. As you sent me into the world, I have sent them into the world. (John 17:14-18). But the false church is very much of this world. It is a political system, sending ambassadors to all nations, functioning as a government. Its leader has always courted favor with kings, premiers, presidents, emperors; has sought to be accepted and liked by them, and has sought to influence them. But Jesus said, "My Kingdom is not of this world: if my Kingdom were of this world then would my servants fight, that I should not be delivered to the Jews: but now is my Kingdom not from hence" (John 18:36). John wrote, "Love not the world, neither the things that are in the world. If any man loves the world, the love of the Father is not in him. "For all that is in the world, the lust of the flesh, and the lust of the eyes, and the pride of life, is not of the Father, but is of the world."And the world passed away and the lust thereof..." (1 John 2:15-17). The word "world" is cosmos, which means the civilization; the communal groupings; cities, governments of the world the society with all its customs, religious and philosophical concepts. God's servants are "citizens" of Christ's soon-coming Heavenly Kingdom, the Government of God! They are like "sojourners" in this world (1 Peter 2:9-12), like "strangers and pilgrims," as if travelers in a foreign country, having no indigenous citizenship. Would an American, traveling in Iraq, fight in Iraq's wars against Iran, or America? Would a Britain, traveling in Africa, vote in African elections, join African military organizations, or observe tribal witchcraft or voodoo? So, God commands His true church to "submit yourselves to every ordinance of man for the Lord's sake: whether it be to the king as supreme; "Or unto governors, as unto them that are sent by him for the punishment of evildoers, and for the praise of them that do well" (1 Peter 2:13-14). So God's servants are to be models in obedience to law, respect for authority; in thankfulness for the freedoms and blessings of the governments under which they live.

They are to obey those governments in every case except where such civil government comes into conflict with the higher court of heaven! In such a case, God's servants must obey God first, and then humbly accept whatever punishment the civil government imposes. Peter and the apostles said to the authorities during their day, "We ought to obey God rather than men!" (Acts 5:29). Christ's true church was never to become a great political system. It was never to fall under the absolute, dictatorial rule of one man, claiming to be the "direct representative" of Christ; claiming to have no peers on earth, but of the many blasphemies of which the great false church is guilty. Any human being arrogating to himself such lofty powers is a stench in the nostrils of God, and will surely answer for the enormity of his folly! It is said that of "Antiochus Epiphanes," the Antichrist of the third kingdom Daniel 8, was the personal enemy of God; so the final Antichrist of the fourth kingdom the final "beast" power, his antitype, shall be. The church has endured a pagan and a papal persecution; there remains for her an infidel persecution...He will not merely, as Popery, substitute himself for Christ in Christ's name, but 'Deny the Father and the Son,' (1 John 2:22). The persecution is to continue up to Christ's second coming". This false prophet claims absolute authority over his followers! They can have no direct access to Christ, and through Christ to the Father, according to his false doctrine! Only when his people stay in his good graces, remain subservient, unquestioning, blind followers of him can they be considered "in the body," and considered as having a spiritual relationship with God. Therefore, this false human leader thinks to usurp the very Priesthood of Christ Himself. He teaches that no man or woman can approach God directly through Christ! They must always be channeled through this one human leader! Finally, this blasphemous and pompous ego will swell to the point that this great false prophet will make the blasphemous claim that he "is God"!

Now, let's notice how this great false church, the "image" of the beast, will be complicit in bringing about the Great Tribulation upon God's elect. Isaiah's prophecy identifies the great false church as a major perpetrator of the tribulation; the captivity of ten-tribes Israel: "I was wroth with my people; I have polluted mine inheritance, and given them into thine hand..." (Isaiah 47:6). This is the fallen woman; the false church, who boasts that she, is "lady of the kingdoms," and will "not suffer the loss of children" who came out of her, in protest. No "rapture" pictured here. Instead, just as Christ predicted; as all the prophecies clearly state, the tribulation is accompanied by a vast martyrdom of saints (Revelation 13:7; Matthew 24:9). To continue, "...thou didst shew them no mercy; upon the ancient hast thou very heavily laid thy yoke" (Isaiah 47:6). Remember, the beast and the false prophet is complicit in the martyrdom of God's people, and in the captivity of the ten-tribes of Israel and Judah! Notice it is not only the great false church that plays her yoke on God's people! Therefore this is what the Lord, the Lord Almighty, says: "My people, who live in Zion, do not be afraid of the Assyrians, who beat you with a rod and lift up a club against you, as Egypt did. Very soon my anger against you will end and my wrath will be directed to their destruction." The LORD Almighty will lash them with a whip, as when he struck down Midian at the rock of Oreb; and he will raise his staff over the waters, as he did in Egypt. In that day their burden will be lifted from your shoulders, their yoke from your neck; the yoke will be broken because you have grown so fat. (Isaiah 10:24-27). Isaiah says, "And it shall come to pass in that day [the time of the end; the time of Christ's coming] that the Lord shall set His hand the second time to recover the remnant of His people, which shall be left, from Assyria...and there shall be an highway for the remnant of His people, which shall be left, from Assyria: LIKE AS IT WAS TO ISRAEL IN THE DAY HE CAME UP OUT OF THE LAND OF EGYPT" (Isaiah 11:11-16). But when the ten-tribes of Israel were taken captive by Assyria in 721-718 BC, your Bible says none returned. There was never a miraculous EXODUS from ancient Assyria. Instead, when Babylon subjugated Assyria, the captive Israelites wandered with their former captors into Europe, and toward Scandinavia and the British Isles.

They disappeared, largely, from history. A few clues remain, and their identity can be discovered, but no such event as that described in Isaiah 11 has yet taken place. Clearly, this prophecy is set at the time of Christ's return. Where is modern Israel the House of Israel, not only the Jews? In captivity, under the yoke of both a modern nation who represents the ancient Assyrians, and the false church! In other words, Israel is under captivity to the beast power and the false prophet! This false prophet is the "little horn" of Daniel the government which finally held sway over the final seven heads of the Roman Empire. This "little horn" of Daniel's prophecy is the papacy, which overthrew three kingdoms which had taken over Rome, generally believed to have been the Vandals (429-533 AD), the Heruli under Odoacer, from the fall of Rome in 476 to about 493, and the eastern Goths from 493 to 554 AD, when General Belesarius retook Carthage. The influence of the papacy was instrumental in overthrowing these kingdoms, and establishing the "Imperial Restoration" of Rome in about 554. Now, the "little horn," speaking great things, thinking to "change times and laws" (establish the Sunday calendar, and issue dogmas), dominates the remaining seven heads of the "beast." These were the successive heads of the so-called "Holy Roman Empire," culminating in the weak revival of the same system under Hitler and Mussolini during World War II. Mussolini called his government the reestablishment of the "Holy Roman Empire"! "The Roman Empire did not represent itself as a continuation of Alexander's; but the Germanic Empire calls itself 'the holy Roman empire". The "Holy Roman Empire" was Germanic, not Italian. Even the first three kings, overthrown by the "little horn," were "Teutonic" people.

John was told, "The beast that you saw was, and is not, and shall ascend out of the bottomless pit [a symbolic "abyss," signifying satanic origin], and go into perdition [so it is the final beast which is ultimately destroyed by Christ's return]" (Revelation 17:8). The leader of this great false church is the FALSE PROPHET of Bible prophecy, the ANTICHRIST! He is the "little horn" of Daniel. He is the "man of sin" of 2 Thessalonians 2. He is the "abomination of desolation" PERSONIFIED, for he is the one who actually will sit in the temple of God, making the blasphemous claim that he is God! Remember how God says the image of the beast, the false church, will have satanic power to perform miracles to delude and deceive millions? Notice! "And then shall that Wicked ["Wicked One,"] be revealed, whom the Lord shall consume with the Spirit of His mouth, and shall destroy with the brightness of His coming: "Even him, whose coming is after the working of Satan with all power and signs and lying wonders, "And will all deceivableness of unrighteousness in them that perish [are perishing]; because they received not the love of the truth, that they might be saved."And for this cause God shall send them strong delusion, that they should believe a lie..." (2 Thessalonians 2:8-11). The false prophet will be seated in a temple. He will claim to be "divine." He will perform such lying wonders, miracles, and mysterious "signs" that millions will be convinced. They will WORSHIP this man; revere him as if he is THE ALMIGHTY GOD! One of the first things Christ will accomplish immediately following His return to this earth is to destroy this great, lying, pompous, blasphemous false prophet. "And the beast was taken [arrested caught], and with him the false prophet that wrought miracles before him, with which he deceived them that had received the mark of the beast, and them that worshipped his image. These both were cast alive into a lake of fire burning with brimstone" In summary, then, Christ specifically said this great "Abomination to God that will cause terrible destruction and desolation," will stand in the holy place, where it ought not! The temple still stood when Christ uttered those words. His listeners knew exactly to which part of the temple He referred: the innermost part of the temple, called the "holy place," which was the place of the priests' daily offerings, and the "holy of holies," behind the Vail, into which the high priest entered only once each year, on the Day of Atonement. Paul clearly said the "man of sin" would sit "in the temple of God." But today, there is no temple in Jerusalem.

Yet, major international tensions occur when enthusiastic Zionist Jews march to the temple walls, attempting to lay a symbolic corner stone for the building of another TEMPLE! The virulent hatred of the Arabs toward the Jews is partly rooted in the intention of many right-wing Jewish sects to destroy the Dome of the Rock and the Al Aksa Mosque, to make way for the building of another Jewish temple. When such a temple is built, be aware that it is NEAR! Consider: Such an event would probably unite the Arab nations as no other single event. A great war could break out in the Mideast a war in which chemical, and even nuclear weapons might be used, for the Arabs might have witnessed the destruction of two of their most revered mosques, holy places to all Islam. They might unite, as never before, and their leader would probably be the "king of the south" of Daniel 11:40-45. To "push at" the "king of the north," who we believe to be the "beast" power, or a United Europe, this Arab leader might cut off all energy to Europe! This would bring an immediate military response as Daniel's 11th chapter shows. If we witness a ten-nation combine in Europe, probably called "The United Nations of Europe," shockingly, suddenly intervene in the Mideast; if we witness the head of the great universal church declare that he is going to MOVE THE VATICAN TO JERUSALEM that the "one true church" is going to go back to its BIRTHPLACE; if we witness him declaring that Jerusalem should become a corpus separatum, or open, internationalized city, exempt from military action, and then GO THERE HIMSELF TO INSURE IT; if we witness miracles performed; major churches, including some state churches returning to the fold of their mother; if we witness this man making great and pompous statements, accepting the acclamation of MILLIONS as the man WHO SAVED THE WORLD FROM NUCLEAR DESTRUCTION; if we witness him revered almost like Christ, acclaimed as if he were "God," then BE WARNED! For, when you see such things happening you should know that the Great Tribulation IS BEGINNING! Should a famous statue that millions have kissed a blackened bronze statue of a figure with a strangely Byzantine or Grecian cast, one who is supposedly the "Peter" of Rome be moved inside the temple; should this man himself ensconce himself inside the temple, then you will have seen the ABOMINATION SET IN PLACE; and horrifying, unimaginable DESTRUCTION will immediately follow!

The consequences of all this to Americans, Britons, Australians, Canadians, South Africans, the democracies of Northwestern Europe, are unimaginable! May God help those whose minds are opened to understand, as Christ said. May God help you to call upon Him for the changes you KNOW you need to make in your life, to repent of sins, to call upon Christ as Savior, and to become a part of His own body, the spiritual organism that is His true church! Christ said "many are called, but few are chosen." Has God called you? Is it an accident you have read this book of witness and warning? Or is God Himself working in your life for a purpose? Think about it. Then, pray about it, while there is still time Black Man. This is a description of death and destruction that has already been set up by GOD long ago before the foundation of the earth to take place soon in time after the Church is removed Black Man, so what's the purpose of your death and destruction upon one another, don't add to "Death, add to "LIFE" "STOP KILLING ME BLACK MAN"

CHAPTER VIII

GEHENNA

"All the references to *Gehenna*, except James 3:6, are from the lips of Christ himself, and there is an obvious emphasis on the punishment for the wicked after death as being everlasting. The term *Gehenna* is derived from the Valley of Hinnom, traditionally considered by the Jews the place of the final punishment of the ungodly. Located just south of Jerusalem, it is referred to in Joshua 15:8 and 18:16, where this valley was considered a boundary between the tribes of Judah and Benjamin. In this place human sacrifices were offered to Molech; these altars were destroyed by Josiah (2 Kings 23:10). The valley was later declared to be 'the valley of slaughter' by Jeremiah (Jer. 7:30-33). The valley was used as a burial place for criminals and for burning garbage. Whatever it's historical and geographic meaning, its usage in the New Testament is clearly a reference to the everlasting state of the wicked, and this seems to be the thought in every instance. In James 3:6 the damage accomplished by an uncontrolled tongue is compared to a fire which 'corrupts the whole person, sets the whole course of his life on fire, and is itself set on fire by hell.' "Christ warned that a person who declares others a fool 'will be in danger of the fire of hell' (Matt. 5:22). In Matthew 5:29 Christ states that it is better to lose an eye than to be thrown into *Gehenna*, with a similar thought regarding it being better to lose a hand than to go into *Gehenna* (Matt. 5:30). In Matthew 10:28 believers in Christ are told not to be afraid of those who kill the body, but rather to 'fear him which is able to destroy both soul and body in hell'.

A similar thought is mentioned in Matthew 18:9, where it is declared better 'to enter life with one eye than to have two eyes and be thrown into the fire of hell.' In Matthew 23:15 Christ denounces the Pharisees who 'travel over land and sea to win a single   convert, and when he becomes one, you make him twice as much a son of hell as you are.' In Matthew 23:33 he denounces the Pharisees and the scribes, asking the question, 'How will you escape being condemned to hell?' In Mark 9:43, 45, 47, the thought recorded in Matthew about it being better to lose part of the body than to be cast into hell is repeated (cf. Matt. 5:22, 29, 30). Luke 12:5 contains a similar thought to that expressed in Matthew 10:28, that one should fear the devil far more than those who might kill them physically. Though not always expressly stated, the implication is that the punishment will have duration and be endless." "In the New Testament the final destination of the wicked is pictured as a place of blazing sulfur, where the burning smoke ascends forever. This would have been an effective image because sulfur fires were part of life for those who lived in the Jerusalem of Bible times. Southwest of the city was the Valley of Hinnom, an area that had a long history of desecration. The steep gorge was once used to burn children in sacrifice to the Ammonite god Molech (2 Kings 23:10; Jer. 7:31; 32:35). Jeremiah denounced such practices by saying that Hinnom Valley would become the valley of God's judgment, a place of slaughter (Jer. 7:32; 19:5-7). As the years passed, a sense of foreboding hung over the valley. People began to burn their garbage and offal there, using sulfur, the flammable substance we now use in matches and gunpowder. Eventually, the Hebrew name *ge-hinnom* (canyon of Hinnom) evolved into *geenna* (*gehenna*), the familiar Greek word for hell (Matt. 5:22, 29; 10:28; 18:9; 23:33; Mark 9:43, 45; Luke 12:5). Thus when the Jews talked about punishment in the next life, what better   image could they use than the smoldering valley they called *Gehenna*? "In the intertestamental period, *gehenna* was widely used as a metaphor for hell, the place of eternal damnation. Later, in rabbinic literature, we find *Gehenna* given a location—in the depths of the earth, and sometimes in Africa beyond the Mountains of Darkness. Some Jews, of course, took the fiery images literally, supposing that Hinnom Valley itself would   become the place of hellfire and judgment (1 Enoch 27:1-2; 54:1-6; 56:3-4; 90:26-28; 4 Ezra 7:36).

But this view was minor and not widely held in Judaism. The New Testament also rejects this view, saying that *Gehenna* is already in some sense prepared elsewhere (Matt. 25:41), just as heaven is (Matt. 25:34; John 14:2; Heb. 11:16)." The name "Gehenna" (Greek, "geena") is a transliteration of the Hebrew "gehinnom", a valley outside of Jerusalem (Josh. 15:8), the exact location of which is uncertain and irrelevant to this study, although generally thought to be somewhere on the south side of the city. In this valley of Hinnom was place called Topeth (2 Kings 23:10) and it is probable that at one time Hinnom and Topeth were both very beautiful and garden-like in their appearance and pleasant places to visit. However, this beautiful valley underwent a change (possibly as early as the reign of Solomon, 1 Kings 11:7) which allowed Jesus to make use of it as a graphic illustration of what the punishment of the lost would be like. The exact meaning of the words "hinnom" and" topeth" are uncertain and various meanings are given to them. But whatever the names mean, it is what happened here that is significant to our study. It was here that the Jews, in their lowest spiritual moments, had practiced every form of idolatry possible (2 Kings 23:10; 2 Chron. 28:3; 33:6; Jer. 7:31; 19:4-5; 32:35) which included the offering of their children in fire to the god "molech". During the reign and reforms of Josiah he had this place "defiled" by tearing down the idols and filling the place with the bones of those who had participated in the idol worship (2 Kings 23:10-14; 2 Chron. 34:4-5), and under Jeremiah the name was changed to what it would now be used for (Jer. 7:31-34; 19:3-6, 10-12). Concerning Hinnom and Topeth, Albert Barnes says "...it was made the place where to throw all of the dead carcasses and filth of the city; and was not infrequently the place of executions. It became, therefore, extremely offensive; the sight was terrific; the air was polluted and pestilential; and to preserve it in any manner pure, it was necessary to keep fires continually burning there. The extreme loathsomeness of the place; the filth and putrefaction; the corruption of the atmosphere, and the lurid fires blazing by day and by night, made it one of the most appalling and terrific objects with which a Jew was acquainted". In the areas of the valley not on fire, scavenger dogs roamed looking for food, and maggots were teeming, feeding on the abundance of rotting matter on which such thrive.

Thus it was that Jesus, when wanting to impress his hearers with the nature of the punishment of the lost, pointed to Gehenna and, by implication, to Topeth. "Gehenna" is used twelve times in the New Testament (Matt. 5:22, 29, 20; 10:28; 18:9; 23:15, 33; Mk. 9:43, 45, 47; Lk. 12:5; Jas. 3:6) eleven times by Jesus Himself, and is the one word that should be translated "hell" for its very derivation connotes every misery and unpleasantness usually associated with all that is "hellish". But "Gehenna" was not the only term employed by Christ and others to describe the nature of punishment. A consideration of these other terms will shed further light upon the nature of the fate of the wicked. "Worm dieth not" (Mk. 9:48). This worm is the maggot already alluded to, "a worm which preys upon dead bodies...The statement signifies the exclusion of the hope of restoration, the punishment being eternal." "Fire and brimstone" (Rev. 21:8) It is probably that "brimstone" originally referred to the gum or resin of trees like cypress or gopher wood, and then "...it was transferred to all inflammable substances, and especially to sulphur...It is exceedingly inflammable, and when burning emits a peculiar suffocating smell" "Unquenchable fire" (Mk. 9:43) Our word "asbestos" comes from this word and means that which is inextinguishable. "Eternal" (Matt. 25:46) Robertson says "The word aionios...means either without beginning or without end of both. It comes as near to the idea of eternal as the Greek can put it in one word". What, then, can be legitimately deduced about the nature of eternal punishment of the lost in Gehenna? THE OLD ENGLISH "hell," denoted that which is covered (hidden or unseen). Consequently, it once served as a suitable translation of the Greek *hades*, which means "imperceptible" or "unseen." In modern English, however, due to the corrupting influence of huma tradition, "hell" has come to mean "the abode of the dead; the place of punishment after death [in which the *dead* are *alive*]." Consequently, since in modern English the notion represented by the term "hell "constitutes, to say the least, interpretation, not translation, it is unconscionable for modern translators to render either the Hebrew *sheol* or the Greek *hades* by this expression. Yet it is worse still, whether in old English or modern English, to render the Greek *tartarosas* and especially the Greek *geenna*, also as "hell."

Such "translations" are not translations at all; they are but the product of circular reasoning and hoary tradition. Whatever one understands may be concerning the matters to which these words make reference, as a *translation* of the Original, the rendering "hell," in all cases, is wholly unjustifiable. Yet it is this very rendering, the single term, "hell," for all these distinct words in the Original, which has spawned all the familiar talk concerning "hell" which prevails among "Bible-believing Christians" today. Just as "anathema," which was originally a cursing formula found in pagan imprecatory texts, was adapted in the Septuagint to represent that which was devoted to destruction (Lev.27:28,29), and was later adapted by the apostle Paul to speak of one who was following a destructive course (Gal.1:8,9), the apostle Peter, as his own figure of likeness, coins the verbal form *tartarosas*, which he adapts from the pagan Greek noun, *Tartaros*, which was the name of the Greek unseen world. It appears in works such as Plato's *Phaedo* and Homer's *Iliad*. It is the name given to the murky abyss deep beneath Hades in which the sins of insurgent and defeated immortals (such as Kronos, or the Titans) are punished. When Peter says that "God spares not sinning messengers," but "[subjects them] to-CAVERNS OF-GLOOM TARTARUS*ing*", "tartarusing" is a coined verbal form used as a figure of speech. In employing this expression, Peter is by no means giving legitimacy to the Greeks' fantastic notions about their unseen world, called Tartarus. Instead, he is simply adapting this word for his own purpose. Since there is a certain *likeness* between that to which God *actually* subjects sinning messengers and that to which the Greeks *imagined* their gods to be subjected in punishment, Peter employs this name for the Greek underworld accordingly. Sinning messengers are decidedly *not* in "Tartarus." Except in the deluded minds of Greek idolators, Tartarus does not exist. Indeed, according to the Scriptures, the sinning messengers are not even said to be undergoing chastening judging at present. Instead, in an estate which may somewhat be likened to the taverns of gloom in the Greeks' fanciful Tartarus, they are said to be *"being kept* for chastening judging" (2 Peter 2:4). Jude adds that "messengers who keep not their own sovereignty, but leave their own habitation, has kept in *imperceptible bonds under gloom* for the judging of the great day" (Jude 6).

Since "chastening" *kolasis* speaks of discipline (i.e., "training"; literally, "hitting") with a view to amendment, we may rejoice that for this they are being kept (cp Heb.12:7-11). In the Scriptures, however, "Gehenna" (hell, AV)—all incredible myths to the contrary notwithstanding does *not* speak of "the place of the eternal torments of the damned." Instead, it refers to an actual place on earth, namely, the valley (or ravine) of Hinnom (Neh.11:30) in the land of Israel. The ravine of Hinnom is a valley to the southwest of Jerusalem (the ravine of the son of Hinnom; Joshua 15:8). The Hebrew phrase *gê* (ravine of) *hinnom* became *geenna* in Greek, whence Gehenna in Latin and English. In time, Moloch, a god worshiped by the Ammonites, came to be worshiped by Israel as well (Lev.18:21; 1 Kings 11:3, 5, 7; 2 Kings 23:10; Amos 5:26; Acts 7:43). In Jeremiah's day, the ravine of Hinnom was associated with the worship of Moloch (Jer.32:35). Josiah, in Judah, defiled this shrine by destroying the high places of Moloch, thus putting a stop to the sacrifices offered there (2 Kings 23:10, 13). Moloch worship incorporated human sacrifice, namely, the sacrifice of children by fire. In the days of the Kings, under Ahaz (2 Chron.28:3) and Manasseh (2 Chron.33:6), children were sacrificed by fire on altars erected within the valley of Hinnom. In later times, according to some, this valley was used for burning the corpses of criminals, animals, and indeed refuses of any sort. Jeremiah spoke of the day when this ravine would no longer be termed the ravine of the son of Hinnom, but rather, the ravine of the killed, and they shall entomb in Tophet because there is no other place (Jer.7: 31,32; cp Jer.12:3; 19:6; Zech.11:4-9). Perhaps this was first carried into effect through the reforms of Josiah (2 Kings 23: 10-20). These considerations rehearse Gehenna's place in the past. It is in Isaiah 66:23, 24, however, that we learn of Gehenna's future role, in the kingdom eon. The book of Isaiah closes with these words, which the Lord Jesus Himself, in the synoptic accounts (Matthew, Mark, and Luke), identifies with Gehenna: The meaning of Gehenna must be established from facts furnished by the Scripture, not by falsehoods foisted by human tradition. To the reader of the Hebrew Scriptures themselves, Gehenna can only mean a verdict which, besides condemning a man to death, also ordains that, after death, his body should be cast into the loathsome valley of Hinnom. This being the sense of Gehenna in the Hebrew Scriptures, we may be sure that this is the sense in which Christ used it. It must be kept in mind, then, as Isaiah 66:23,24 makes clear, that in the era of Israel's restoration, the judging of Gehenna (Matt.23:33) will be instituted. In the stated seasons of worship, representatives of the nations who will come to Jerusalem, will go forth and see the *corpses of the mortals* who transgressed the law in such a way so as to be subjected to death. Their corpses will remain unburied: worms will prey upon the corrupting flesh, and fires will always be at work to purify the air from pestilential infection. Gehenna" appears in the Greek   Scriptures twelve times (Matt.5:22,29,30; 10:28; 18:9; 23:15,33; Mark 9:43,45,47; Luke 12:5; James 3:6). Not one of these passages has reference to the so-called final state. The Lord explicitly identifies Gehenna with Isaiah 66:23,24 by speaking of it as the place of unextinguished fire, where their worm is not deceasing and the fire is not going out (Mark 9:46). All whose bodies are destroyed in Gehenna will be raised to be judged at the great white throne, and go into the lake of fire. Gehenna is the capital punishment of the kingdom, without burial. In Matthew 10:28 the Lord declares: And do not fear those who are killing the body, yet are not able to kill the soul. Yet fear Him, rather, Who is able to destroy the soul as well as the body in Gehenna. Since, as explained in the previous exposition, The Soul and the Unseen, we know that soul speaks of sensation, and that in death there is no sensation, we will not imagine that the reason why man is not able to kill the soul is because the soul is immortal. Besides, since, as this very passage plainly states, *God* is able to destroy the soul, we will be certain that the soul is *not* immortal. In this phrase, then, not able to kill the soul, kill is figurative, and is a relative statement with reference not to their present life, but to their life in the coming ages. With reference to the delights of the kingdom, those who would kill one of these faithful ones, would not be able to hinder (put a stop to, or kill) the bliss which they will enjoy in that day.

Those who come under God's judgment in the Messiah's kingdom will not only have their bodies destroyed in the valley of Hinnom, but they will be subjected to total loss (destruction) of the joys which their souls long for in the kingdom. The martyrs who die for the sake of the kingdom have nothing to fear. So far as their souls [their sensations] are concerned, death gives them an immediate entrance into the delights of the earthly paradise, even though at their martyrdom it was thousands of years in the future. The fact that a fire is inextinguishable (Matt.3:12; Mark 9:43), does not entail its burning for all eternity. It does not follow that a fire which is not put out will never go out. After rebuking Israel for her sins and idolatry, Yahweh declared that He would pour out His indignation upon Jerusalem, on man and beast, on the trees of the field and on the fruit of the ground: it shall burn and shall not be quenched" (Jer.7:20). This was fulfilled in the Babylonian captivity. The fires of that day burned themselves out long ago. Surely the fires of Gehenna, if indeed they are still burning at that time, will themselves be consumed by fire, in the day, following the thousand years, in which the earth's elements are dissolved by combustion (2 Peter 3:10). Similarly, the fact that "the Gehenna of fire (Matt.18:8, 9) affords us no reason to claim that it is an endless fire, and, therefore, that it is a fire that is to be identified with so-called "everlasting punishment. Indeed, the fact that, following the kingdom, the valley of Gehenna, together with the entire earth, will be dissolved by combustion (2 Peter 3:10-13; Rev.20:11; 21:1), proves that Gehenna fire is *not* everlasting fire. The weeping and gnashing of teeth which are usually associated with it, in fact, have no connection with Gehenna. This expression usually occurs in connection with outer darkness, quite the opposite of the lurid flames of Gehenna. Even so, since this fearful phrase is so often predicated of the final condition of the damned, it will be worthwhile to put it where it belongs. In Matthew 8:12, our Lord, commenting on the faith of the centurion said, yet the sons of the kingdom shall be cast out into outer darkness. There shall be lamentation and gnashing of teeth.

The kingdom (the kingdom of the heavens) is likened to a wedding (Matthew 22:2-14). The sons are Israelites *according to the flesh.* Just as an unfit guest would be thrust out into the dark night, while within the marriage feast was being enjoyed in brilliant light, so it will be for certain living Israelites who seek to enter the kingdom on earth. Among those who remain alive after the time of Jacob's trouble (Jer.30:7), the great affliction" (Matt.24:21), will be some who while not overtly lawless nonetheless are unworthy of the kingdom. They will continue to live, yet be barred from it. They will have no part in the wedding festivities, that is, in the glorious reign which will be centered in Jerusalem. Accordingly, they will lament and gnash their teeth in the day when they see Abraham and Isaac and Jacob and all the prophets in the kingdom of God, while they themselves are cast outside (Luke 13:28; Matt. 22:11-13; 25:30). Before the kingdom, however, in the concluding period of the present age, the Son of Mankind will send His messengers to be culling out of His kingdom all the *snares* and those *doing lawlessness,* and they shall be casting *them* into a furnace of fire. There shall be lamentation and gnashing of teeth (Matt.13: 41, 42). In the nature of the case, lamentation and gnashing of teeth, here, must be confined to those who while observers of this judgment nonetheless are not among its subjects, as well as to those wicked ones among its subjects, who, through circumstances, find it impossible to avoid the contemplation of their own imminent doom. The figure is that of clearing a field for planting. Many will be destroyed, some by literal fire (Rev.9:17, 18; 16:8; 18:8, 18). Matthew 13:49 limits this judgment to the conclusion of the present age. Under the Circumcision evangel, personal righteousness according to law is essential to life in the kingdom. Only those working righteousness may enter into life. Nevertheless, the chosen ones, who, indeed, are worthy, are only so according to the choice of grace (Rom.11:5). They *will* be saved, yet not apart from an upright walk. Though they *will* endure, still, they *must* endure in order either to enter the kingdom without dying or to be worthy of the resurrection of the just.

The salvation of the Circumcision, which though *through* works *accords* with *grace*, nonetheless does not accord with fatalism. Hence, in all gravity, the Lord warns even His own disciples of the judging of Gehenna which will come upon *all* capital transgressors. All of this is contrary to the grace which we enjoy today as members of the body of Christ, through the evangel proclaimed by the apostle Paul. We are not under law (Rom.6:14); we are justified apart from law (Rom.3:21, 24); life itself is a gracious gift (Rom.6:23). Indeed, in our case, if sin should be increasing, grace will super exceed (Rom.5:20). This is not true concerning the chosen under the evangel of the Circumcision, but it is true concerning those who are chosen according to the evangel of the Uncircumcision. Gehenna fire only concerns the transgressors of Moses law in the coming kingdom on earth. It has no reference whatever to the members of the body of Christ, nor to the final destiny of the lost. It is confined to the coming age and to the nation of Israel in that day.

A Message to the Black Man

All men reason from certain premises according to their intellectual mine set. So do the animals, and each man or animal shows his development as plain as his color. The Ethiopian cannot change his skin, or the leopard his spots. This figure is to show that a man in his reasoning cannot make himself wiser or clearer than he started at first. If his wisdom is as black as the Ethiopian's skin, he cannot make it white by his argument and if it is spotted by the corruption of a demagogue, his reason cannot wash out the spots. A writer is known by his fruits of Labor. He begins by saying that all men must admit that the creator is wiser than the creature. Then he assumes what he does not confine himself to. God made the Black Man but not to be enslaved, but the Black Man seems to make God the author of slavery by identifying to both death and destruction. The Bible says, GOD made the Black Man in his own image. The writer says that the White Man and the Black Man are both of the human species, it is foolish to deny, but that they are unlike in color and capacity, it is no less foolish to deny. Now if the White Man and the Black Man are both of the human species, how did the black man become enslaved by the white man?

But I will return to the creator. According to His own reasoning, He admits that color has   nothing to do with species, so we class all colors of men together with equal rights. Everyone knows that might is right with the animals, so it must have been the case in the early ages of mankind, for all beings admit this law by their action. No one supposes that God put one class under another, neither is it supposable that what is wisdom in one race is not so in another. Here is where things differ from the races; in many White Men's eyes God makes one man superior to another, but in "The Kingdom" GOD makes all men alike. Now there is nothing simpler than that they are not alike, then how comes this absurdity? Because it is in us and not in God. Creation and formation are not alike. If God created man in his own image, it cannot be that He had reference to what we see with our natural eyes.

They *will* be saved, yet not apart from an upright walk. Though they *will* endure, still, they *must* endure in order either to enter the kingdom without dying or to be worthy of the resurrection of the just. The salvation of the Circumcision, which though *through* works *accords* with *grace*, nonetheless does not accord with fatalism. Hence, in all gravity, the Lord warns even His own disciples of the judging of Gehenna which will come upon *all* capital transgressors. All of this is contrary to the grace which we enjoy today as members of the body of Christ, through the evangel proclaimed by the apostle Paul. We are not under law (Rom.6:14); we are justified apart from law (Rom.3:21, 24); life itself is a gracious gift (Rom.6:23). Indeed, in our case, if sin should be increasing, grace will super exceed (Rom.5:20). This is not true concerning the   chosen under the evangel of the Circumcision, but it is true concerning those who are chosen according to the evangel of the Uncircumcision. Gehenna fire only concerns the transgressors of Moses law in the coming kingdom on earth. It has no reference whatever to the members of the body of Christ, nor to the final destiny of the lost. It is confined to the coming age and to the nation of Israel in that day. Appears that the black man is inferior to the white man, but then he cannot be so dangerous. It is the duty of every man to relieve his fellow man from the burdens that bind him down. You may not have your dog eat at the same table with yourself, but in your wisdom, you ought to respect his position and not despise him because he is not as good as you are, and you should rejoice that he is contented. There is a vast difference between a man being a slave and being a servant. This difference cannot be seen by plain development, is not up to that standard, and if it were not for the GOD's wisdom that makes this difference, no one would see the difference between the poor whites and the black slave, for he makes no distinction except in name. Everyone knows that you can find all grades of intellect from the ignorant up to the intellectual in the white race. Then why should not the same intellect is branded as well in the black race? The mode of reasoning shows development, that intellect is kept in check by a wisdom superior to one's own, which does not come outside of one's own opinions. It is said the most ignorant being is either black or blind, and as he grows wise he becomes spotted.

This is the demagogue and his wisdom is his reason, but he is wise only in his own conceit. True wisdom rules by GOD, false wisdom by opinion, and when we see a person set himself up as wiser or a dictator, and then you may know that his wisdom is of this world of opinion. But when man can see that God never made one Kingdom/or earthly truth to tyrannize over another of the same combination, then you will see a man that is not of opinion. Slavery, black or white, is the offspring of opinions, like the earth; and when the earth becomes enriched by the wisdom of science, it brings forth fruits (like freedom), but in its original state, it brings forth only briars and thorns. So with the development of man. As he becomes wise, he loses the earthly, overbearing or brutal man, and sees that wisdom is the true man and not color or opinions, that which the Black Man can put into practice. Then he respects each man black and white for what he knows; and instead of making himself popular by deceiving the masses death and destruction, he can practice elevating other men by his wisdom, breaking down the bars of oppression and letting the minds of men live and feed in the sound pastures of knowledge, understanding and wisdom. Like David, he will lead the people along by the voice of his wisdom and he will not teach them to forge chains to bind their fellow man, giving God the praise that they are not slaves or murderers like their neighbors. This kind of slavery is demagoguism. It appeals only to one set of slaves to rule the other, and is on a level with the thief that enters the African shores and sets the black tribes to fighting, killing and then making money out of the quarrel, telling them that God never intended that those who can be subdued should have their freedom. The same theory would carry out and be applied to every nation on earth. It is not one black man upon the killing of another black man above the lowest treason of the black-hearted nature of the South, and it is in keeping with his life and acts, whoever he may be, you will find him popular with one kind of slaves just as any negro thief is popular with those who will sell their race into slavery. Many stands to be honest but so are the wolf who steals the sheep for his own eating. The two are both brutes, one a little higher than the other.

Neither has any claim to an intellectual mind but show just how far they have advanced from ignorance into error on the road to wisdom. So he is to be looked upon, not as a fool but as a man of opinions, and not to be classed with that refined class of intellect that judges every one by his acts. Then he becomes a harmless serpent whose bite will not poison the multitude. The trouble with all such demagogues is that error and hypocrisy usually go hand in hand, and persons keep out of sight the very object they wish to attain. This is the case with the brute "Black Man". His aim is selfish and not honest; therefore he keeps out of sight the progress of the higher intellect because he believes it can't be appreciated. So he gives way to the evil in his heart, and like Judas sells his higher wisdom for a petty office or popularity with the masses. Like Nebuchadnezzar, weighed in the balance and found wanting, he shows which end of the scale he is on. His god is one of his own mistakes, like all others who wish to dictate the masses by their own opinion. My God speaks in this way. He has finished his work and sits down to see it work, it needs no repairs, it will run and perform its work, till every one shall know that to be good is to be wise and man's color is not the problem of oppression but lack of wisdom. And wisdom when reduced to practice will be recognized by every wise and benevolent person without regard to color. Slavery and Death is one of the very first acts of man, at least it is an element as necessary as any other evil. It was intended by the creator for a wise purpose, but it never will be looked upon by a scientific mind as containing any of the elements of wisdom. It is the yeast in the lump of wisdom that agitates the mind or matter to bring out this great truth that man is capable of governing himself and that all will submit to GOD's wisdom when it is shown, either in the white man or black man.

So slavery and Death is one of the evils that is necessary to show man the error of his own way, and teach him that so long as he is capable of enslaving and murdering his fellow man, he is digging a pit that he may at some point in time fall into himself. Look at the progression of "Honor & Freedom" ever since the world began and you will see just how far the bonds have been broken and the tongue of wisdom and liberty let loose. The two elements have always existed by a variety of names. Error at first was called the serpent, then the devil, and has always had it as a foot stool. Everyone knows that when a person tries to palm off an error as mathematical science, he shows the weak part of his wisdom or his cloven foot. This "Black Man" has shown and will always show in every communication or act of violence he can, till he is exposed and sees that his hypocrisy can be detected by the wisdom of GOD in the masses of the righteous. Then he will cease from doing evil and learn to be honest and do well. The Unrighteous Black Man like many others of the same stripe will never cease from his hypocritical reasoning till his errors are exposed. The wisdom is in his strategy and his strategy is in his deception. Murder is the case that they gave him. STOP KILLING ME BLACK MAN!!!

Choose to be Black Man

If you think of yourself to be a murderer, than you think right. Any man who hates his brother GOD says is a murderer. No matter what has brought you to where you are, it is up to you to choose to be. Has any principle powers beyond your control force you not to be or held you up? Absolutely so! Do you know how to move forward from such powers to be? Do you want to move forward from such a strong hold?

Though others may be to blame for who you've become, you are accountable. Though you may have many reasons to feel pity for yourself, it will not add one day to your life. If you see yourself as a victim, it is because you have chosen to be a victim.

Is that hardcore and no love? Then focus on this. There are many who have suffered much more than you, who have chosen not to be a victim, who has chosen instead to live life as it should be. You can choose to be accountable and by doing so you can choose to be.....Black Man!

Rev. Anthony Martin—

20 TIME AUTHOR

INSPIRATIONAL/MOTIVATIONAL

SPEAKER

THE KINGDOM CULTURE FELLOWSHIP MINISTRIES
&
CHRISTIAN SELF PUBLISHING CO.

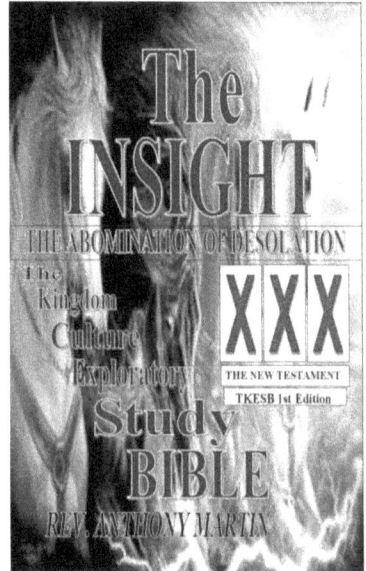

THE KINGDOM CULTURE EXPLORATORY

STUDY BIBLE

THE KINGDOM ENGLISH STANDARD BIBLE

www.ingramcontent.com/pod-product-compliance
Lightning Source LLC
Chambersburg PA
CBHW031202270326
41931CB00006B/372